Wetlands

Wetlands

MARYLIN LISOWSKI
and
ROBERT A. WILLAIMS

FRANKLIN WATTS
A Division of Grolier Publishing
New York   London   Hong Kong   Sydney
Danbury, Connecticut

Note to Readers: Terms defined in the glossary are bold in the text.

Photographs ©: Corbis-Bettmann: 50, 51; Photo Researchers: 55, 70 (Jack Dermid), 89 (Lowell Georgia), 27 (Karl H. Maslowski), 95 (C. G. Maxwell), 15 (Tom McHugh), 57 (Omikron), 30, 31 (M. W. F. Tweedie), 65 (Jerome Wexler); Visuals Unlimited: 97 (John Sohlden).
Illustrations by Vantage Art, Inc.
Book interior design and pagination by Carole Desnoes

Library of Congress Cataloging-in-Publication Data

Lisowski, Marylin.
    Wetlands / Marylin Lisowski and Robert A. Williams
        p. cm. — (Exploring ecosystems)
    Summary: Provides instructions for projects and activities that explore
the five major types of wetlands and demonstrate why they are valuable.
    Includes bibliographical references and index.
    ISBN 0-531-11344-5
    1. Wetland ecology—Study and teaching—Activity programs—Juvenile
literature. [1. Wetland ecology—Experiments. 2. Ecology—Experiments.
3. Wetlands—Experiments. 4. Experiments.] I. Williams, Robert A., 1940- .
II. Title. III. Series.
QH541.5.M3L48 1997   96-25739
574.5'26325—dc20   CIP
                                                                   AC

To my Mom; my sisters, Marya and Rosie;
my brothers, Joseph, Paul, Antos, John, and Michael;
my nieces and nephews; and my friend, Bob.

M. L.

To Sissy, Shawn, Big and Little Jeff,
JoAnn and Wally, and my friend, Marylin

R. A. W.

Contents

Wetlands

Introduction

DO YOU KNOW WHAT THE FLORIDA Everglades, the Arctic tundra, and prairie potholes in Minnesota have in common? They are all **wetlands**. What exactly is a wetland? That question is not so easy to answer. There are many types of wetlands, and legal definitions may differ from scientific ones. Even though the definition of a wetland has gone through many changes, it is generally agreed that each type of wetland possesses distinct hydrologic (water), geomorphic (soil), chemical, and biological features. The activities in this book will help you understand what wetlands are and why they are so special.

To be considered a wetland, a region must have water-saturated soils or be covered by a shallow layer of water for at least part of the year. The United States Fish and Wildlife Service, a branch of the Department of the Interior, has developed a classification system for wetland areas. The major groupings are listed below. How many types of wetlands do you think can be found in your area?

11

- **Marine wetlands** are found along the edges of the ocean. They are constantly exposed to salty ocean water. Tidal pools, mudflats, and open beach areas form the major features of marine wetlands.
- **Estuarine wetlands** occur in areas where fresh water and salt water mix. Large areas along the southeastern coast of the United States and the Florida Gulf coast are examples of such habitats.

  The saline content of the **salt marshes** and **mangrove swamps** in these areas allows them to support a rich network of life. Salt marshes are dominated by grasses or grasslike plants. Mangrove swamps form in areas with warm water. They are common on islands in the Gulf Stream and the Gulf of Mexico as well as along the southern Florida coast.
- **Riverine wetlands** lie along the borders of rivers and streams. Great riverine wetlands were once prominent along every North American river. Eighty percent or more of the wetlands along the Missouri and Mississippi Rivers have been destroyed.
- **Lacustrine wetlands** are associated with lakes, ponds, and reservoirs. These wetland areas may extend from the shoreline out to a depth of 2 meters (6 ft.). These wetlands include lakeside **bogs** and marshes. Aquatic beds of submerged or floating plants are usually present in this type of wetland.
- **Palustrine wetlands** are found in forested areas. This is by far the most diverse type of wetland. It includes the Arctic tundra, wet prairies, sedge meadows, fresh meadows, inland swamps and marshes, flood plains, fens, bogs, and seasonally flooded basins.

  Sedge meadows contain large numbers of grasslike plants, while fresh meadows have broad-leafed plants. In many cases, fresh meadows have wet soils, but are not inundated with water.

  In shrub swamps, which form in areas that will not support large trees, Alders, dogwoods, and willows may form impenetrable shrub jungles. Wooded swamps, which are dominated by either **coniferous** or hardwood trees, are wet most of the year. They are generally associated with ancient lake basins or old river **oxbows**. They retain storm water and support a diverse array of wildlife. Hardwood swamps often support cypress, ash, maple, birch, or white cedar trees, while mature conifers are found in the coniferous swamps.

Flood-plain forests are found close to rivers. They are characterized by **alluvial** soil that has been deposited by flooding waters. Hardwoods such as maples, pecans, river birches, and ashes are common. In addition, cottonwoods or sycamores are often present. Flood plains often dry up during the late summer.

Seasonally flooded basins are poorly drained, shallow depressions that may have standing water for very brief periods each year. During dry periods, these areas may be cultivated. Prairie potholes, one type of seasonally flooded basin, were formed by glaciers as they moved across and scoured the land. Prairie potholes in Montana, North Dakota, South Dakota, and Minnesota are North America's most productive waterfowl regions. In the fall, the potholes serve as stopover sites for migrating birds. In the spring, they host nesting waterfowl. Prairie potholes are dominated by grasses, although cattails may be present.

Calcareous fens form around springs with calcium-and mineral-laden water. Open bogs support mosses as well as broad-leafed evergreens and some shrubs.

The coniferous bogs and swamps found in wet northern forests may be highly acidic and often contain mosses as well as large and small evergreens. Bogs are characterized by an accumulation of **peat**, a rich organic material that has been built up and compressed over time. The plants that grow in bogs are adapted to high acidity and low oxygen levels. Many bogs are covered with a spongy mat of **sphagnum moss**. Because decomposition in bogs is very slow, plants and animals that fall into these areas often remain well preserved for thousands of years. Who knows what you may find as you search through a local bog.

The Wealth of Wetlands

Can you imagine having a great treasure in your possession and not even realizing it? At one time, wetlands were though to be undesirable places that should be drained or filled. Not until the 1960s did ecologists and concerned citizens begin to recognize the importance of the wetlands. Wetlands are a significant source of food and water. They serve as temporary and permanent homes for a tremendous variety of wildlife. Wetlands also act as flood barriers, prevent erosion, and provide recreational enjoyment.

It is estimated that you can find more animals and plants per hectare or acre in a wetland than in almost any other kind of **ecosystem**. Most of the fish and shellfish we eat begin their lives in wetlands, where thick vegetation protects them from predators. Wetlands also attract migrating birds, such as ducks, eagles, and geese. As these birds travel north in the spring and south in the fall, they use wetlands as nighttime stopover sites. About 43 percent of all the animals and plants classified as endangered or threatened depend on wetlands. Examples include bald eagles, American crocodiles, whooping cranes, and wood storks.

Wetlands are also important recreational sites for humans. Many people enjoy canoeing, hiking, and exploring in wetlands, and more than 50 million people observe and photograph birds in wetland areas every year. These vacationers spend about $10 million annually. In addition, wetlands support a multibillion-dollar fishing industry.

Wetlands serve as cleaning agents for polluted water. Wetland plants, which absorb and break down chemicals and impurities, prevent pollutants from moving into— and contaminating—rivers, groundwater, and other

The American alligator, North America's largest reptile, is a common sight in the Everglades National Park in Florida. Alligators, which were nearly hunted to extinction earlier this century, may also be spotted in wetlands as far north as the Carolinas and as far west as Texas. They are major predators and scavengers in swamps and along rivers.

sources of drinking water. In addition, the roots and stems of wetland plants retain silt and sediment, preventing them from traveling farther downstream.

In recent years, scientists have designed artificial wetlands to filter water that comes into town and city sewage-treatment systems. Wetland organisms are introduced to remove toxic materials or wastes from the sewage. As water flows from these human-made marshes, sediment and chemicals are removed and water quality is improved.

Wandering Through the Wetlands

I f you live near the ocean, you should be able to find all five types of wetland near your home. If you live inland, you will probably be able to find and visit riverine, lacustrine, and palustrine wetlands.

Before you begin to explore wetland ecosystems, you need to know how to locate a wetland. Maps are a good place to start. Many **topographical maps** will show you the locations of wetland areas. Once you are in the vicinity of a wetland, look around and ask yourself the following questions:

- Are there plants with floating leaves?
- Is the soil wet or is there evidence that it was once wet?
- Is the area saturated with water?
- Do reedlike plants grow in or close to the area?

If you can answer yes to all of these questions, you have found the perfect study site. Before you begin to explore, think about keeping records. How do you want to keep track of what you find?

Reflecting, Recording, and Remembering

P hotographs and drawings are excellent ways to record what you observe in a wetland. You will want to keep some written records of your findings, too.

A field journal is the best way to record all the sights, sounds, feelings, and findings associated with your wetland adventure. Journal entries can help you compare one wetland area to another. Most scientists record their observations in a journal, usually a sturdy notebook, with some type of permanent marking pen. Scientists who do outdoor research often keep their journal in a plastic resealable bag to protect it from rain and other types of moisture.

The entries in your field journal should consist of a list of the physical and biological events that you witness as you experience them. It might include drawings of the plants and animals you encounter, photographs of the site, and completed data sheets (Figure 1).You may want to make photocopies of Figure 1 on the next page to use as you explore wetland ecosystems. When you get home, you can add some general information about how what you saw and experienced in the wetland affected you.

You might want to include some of the following data in your journal:

- date, time, and location;
- weather conditions (temperature, wind direction and speed, relative humidity, cloud conditions);
- plant-life observations (types, numbers, descriptions);
- animal-life observations (types, numbers, distribution, behaviors, adaptations);
- surrounding area (land-use patterns, special features, odors);
- soil conditions (water saturation, soil type, erosion); and
- anything that seemed special or unusual.

While your field journal is your most important piece of equipment, some of the activities in this book call for other kinds of equipment. You will find directions for constructing these devices in the Appendix at the back of this book.

The information in this introduction should provide you with all of the knowledge you need to identify an area as a wetland. Once you choose and locate a wetland site near your home, you can perform the activities and experiments described throughout this book. As you begin to explore, be sure to bring along your adventurous spirit and be ready to enjoy the wonder of the wetlands.

Figure 1 Sample Data Sheet of Wetland Characteristics

Name of Observer _____ Wetlands Location _____ Date _____

Physical Features
Temperature
  soil _____
  air _____
  water _____

Wind
  direction _____
  speed _____

cloud conditions _____

relative humidity _____

Soil
  moisture _____
  color _____

Land use
  human alterations _____
  nearby uses _____

Water Environment
  shore Observations _____
  depth of Water _____

Biotic Features
Soil Life Forms
  ☐ worms
  ☐ larvae
  ☐ insects
  ☐ animals homes

Plant Populations
At Water's Edge
  ☐ reeds
  ☐ sedges
  ☐ rushes
  ☐ grasses

Broad-leafed Plants (underwater)
  ☐ waterlilies
  ☐ pondweeds

Fine-leafed Plants (underwater)
  ☐ plants with leaves in whorls
  ☐ branching plants

Trees
  number _____
  types _____

Animal Populations
At Water's Edge
  ☐ burrows and holes
  ☐ nests

Animal Signs
  ☐ droppings
  ☐ markings

Animal Sightings
  number _____
  types _____

On (or in) the Ice
Macroorganisms
  number _____
  types _____

Microorganisms
  number _____
  types _____

CHAPTER 1

What's Wild in the Wetlands

HAVE YOU EVER WONDERED WHAT IT would be like to go on a wildlife safari? What would you do there? What would you expect to encounter? What would be a good site for a safari? How about a wetland?

Many unique and unusual animals live in wetland areas. You can find more animals and plants per hectare or acre in a wetland than in almost any other kind of habitat. Although some wetland animals may be quite familiar to you, you will come to know many others as you explore wetlands.

What kinds of sounds, sights, smells, and movements can you expect on a wetland wildlife safari? You may be surprised at all you experience as you begin to investigate what's wild in the wetlands.

Where and when can you expect to see some of the most common wetland in-

19

habitants? Different kinds of animals are found in different regions of a wetland. Since water is a very important factor in the wetlands, it can be used as a starting point for scouting animals. As you begin your explorations, you will discover that specific animals can be found near the water. Others are generally located on the water; still others live under the water. This chapter offers suggestions for examining the life forms found in these three locations.

Because the time when you perform an investigation may influence your results, always remember to record the time and date in your field journal. If possible, visit the same wetland area at different times of the day and during different seasons of the year. Compare your observations. Did you notice any differences? Can you explain these differences?

Animals Near the Water

To many animals, the water's edge is a source of safety as well as a source of food. This makes it a great place to find animals. However, observing animals near the water may not be as easy as it seems. Many creatures hide among the plants that grow close to the shore. It's a good idea to wear clothes that help you blend in with the landscape and to avoid making sudden movements that could scare away the animals. Also, keep wind direction in mind. Mammals will be less likely to detect your scent if you stay downwind.

Just as you tend to eat and sleep at certain times, so do animals. For example, raccoons are usually active at night, while many species of frogs are active at dusk or dawn. If you want to observe these animals, visit a local wetland site at night. Next, take some time to learn the habits of the animals you wish to study. For example, would you expect to see a deer in broad daylight or would you have a better chance of observing a red-winged blackbird? A **wildlife inventory** will provide the answer.

Studying animals that live near the water takes some planning and persistence, but it is worth the effort. The following activities will help you to become a skilled wetlands explorer.

Counting Critters:
How to Inventory Wildlife

How do we know that a particular kind of animal lives in a wetland area? We know because someone has seen it there and recorded its presence. The process of counting and recording wildlife is a basic procedure for many scientists and naturalists. A wildlife inventory can provide a great deal of information about a specific area. By conducting your own inventory, you will learn which animals come to the water regularly and which have the largest populations. You will also discover how these animals go about their daily lives.

Animals that spend most of their time searching for food in fields and forests gather near the water's edge regularly. You will see this if you are patient and observant. One way to recognize the movement of animals to the water's edge is by completing a survey at different times of the day. Eventually you will discover why and when these animals come to the water.

When you have determined the animals' daily schedules, do a seasonal survey that will tell you which animals live in your wetland area year-round and which are **migratory** (stop on the way to another destination).

What changes can you expect in different seasons? In the autumn, most wetland areas are full of migratory waterfowl, such as ducks, geese, herons, and egrets. In winter, a northern wetland may have few inhabitants. Year-round residents, such as chickadees or blue jays, make good subjects for food- or nesting-preference studies.

By repeating your inventory periodically, you can note any

changes taking place in the animal community that relies on the wetland. Changes in numbers can provide clues about the overall health of the wetland ecosystem. For instance, scientists all over the world have observed that amphibians, such as frogs and salamanders, are disappearing from wetlands. What does this tell you? Are amphibians abundant in your wetland area?

If your wetland is in a city park, you may notice that the presence of humans affects the behavior of other animals. On which day of the week do humans have the greatest impact on animals visiting the water's edge?

Begin your wildlife inventory by making a map of the wetland area. Show the location of the animals and indicate whether they move around or stay in one place. You can draw a separate map for each observation date or you can simply use different-colored pencils to indicate different observation times.

An inventory requires you to list all the animals you see in a specific wetland area. One way to do this is to locate the animal on a map of the wetland observation site and then transfer the animals' names to a table for counting and comparison. See Table 1. The table is a continuing summary of your observations. Both a map and a table can provide you with a profile of the types of animals that make their homes in your wetland area.

If you keep this list as long as you observe the wetland

Table 1   Wetland Inventory

Mammals	Birds	Insects/ Spiders	Reptiles	Amphibians
Raccoon (date)	Great egret (date)	Dragonfly (date)	Turtle (date)	Bullfrog (date)
White-tailed deer (date)				

area, you will have a valuable record of the wildlife there. As the seasons change, you can add new arrivals and note absences. You can also expand your list as you learn the names of unfamiliar animals and learn to differentiate species that look very much alike.

Don't be concerned if it takes you quite a bit of practice to identify some animals. Many amphibians and birds have similar features. For example the piping plover and the killdeer may initially look the same to you, but with continued observations, their distinguishing characteristics will become more apparent. The red-winged blackbird can also be tricky to identify because the male and female look so different. First observations might lead you to believe they are two different species of birds. If you are persistent, the benefits and joys of careful observation will be yours.

On the Right Track: How to Make an Animal Cast

Did you ever think that nature exploration is like detective work? Sometimes the best evidence for the presence of wildlife comes from clues such as an animal track. As you explore the areas along the wetland's edge, you will discover all kinds of evidence left behind by animals: a piece of fur, a partially eaten leaf, a broken twig, or a track. You may want to collect these clues and organize them into a wetland mini-museum.

If you find an animal track in the mud, you can make an impression—or cast—of it and then try to identify the animal that made it. If you arrive at a wetland area at dawn or at dusk, you may see deer tracks. Deer come to the water's edge to drink every day.

To make a cast of an animal track, you will need several plastic or flexible cardboard strips measuring 6 centimeters

× 26 centimeters (2 in. × 10 in.), plaster of paris in a small resealable bag, a container for mixing the plaster (cut a 2-liter plastic soda bottle in half), a paper cup, a sponge, a paper clip, and a stick.

Once you have found a track, ask yourself the following questions: Is the print well defined? Is the soil around the track firm enough to hold the plaster of paris? Is there enough room to make a cast (the track may be in a hard-to-reach place)? If the answers to these questions are yes, it's time to get to work.

Begin by clearing all the leaves, small sticks, and rocks away from the track. If the track is covered with a layer of water, use the sponge to soak it up. (Adding plaster of paris to this excess water will not work.)

Shape the piece of plastic or cardboard into a circle around the track. The plastic should be about 3 to 4 centimeters (1 to 1.5 in.) away from the track's edge. You do not have to make a perfect circle, just surround the track so that the plaster of paris will not run. If the circular dam opens easily, fasten the ends with the paper clip, as shown in Figure 2. You may need to push the cylinder into the ground a bit to make a tight seal.

Using a strong stick, mix the plaster with water until it is runny. (Remember to take the stick home with you. You cannot discard it in the wetland.) You will have to decide how thin the mixture should be based on how much time you have and how wet the soil is. The thinner the plaster mixture, the longer it will take to harden. (Hint: The mixture should probably be about the same thickness as runny pancake batter.) You will also have to decide how much of the mixture to make. (You cannot discard the excess in the wetland, it will harden in the container. If you use the bottom of a 2-liter soda bottle, you can discard the excess mixture at home.) **Never wash the container out in a sink. The excess can harden in the water pipes and block them.**

When the plaster of paris and water are thoroughly mixed, carefully pour the mixture into the mold. Fill the mold halfway to the top (the plaster shape or cast should be sev-

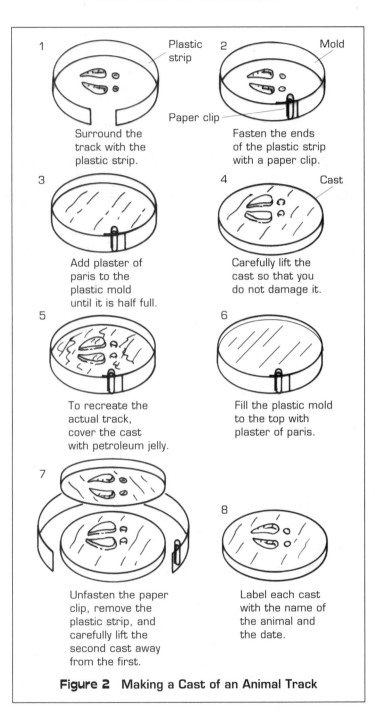

Figure 2 Making a Cast of an Animal Track

eral centimeters thick). Allow the cast to harden. Don't hurry this step unless it begins to rain. If the cast is too soft, it will not solidify and the track will be ruined. If you cannot wait, put a sheet of plastic over the cast to protect it and come back later.

The hardened cast is not easily damaged, but be gentle when pulling up the cast and plastic mold. Check to see if the cast captured the track properly, and wash it off with water to remove any excess soil. What you have captured is a model of the hoof or foot that made the track, not the actual track as you found it.

To re-create the actual track at home, make a cast of the model you created at the wetland. First, slide the plastic mold you made earlier over the cast and cover the surface of your cast with petroleum jelly. Pour a new layer of plaster of paris into the mold. After the plaster has hardened completely, remove the mold and lift the second cast.

The second cast should look just like the track you saw in the wetland. You now have a copy of the original track and a copy of the foot of the animal that made the track. Label each cast with the name of the animal and the date the cast was made. What a masterpiece and what a great way to remember your visit!

PROJECT 3

Wing Patrol:
How to Record Bird Behaviors

Red-winged blackbirds, which nest in the reeds and cattails along the water's edge, can provide many hours of interesting observation.

Male red-winged blackbirds are easy to spot because they sport brilliant red and yellow shoulder patches. They arrive at wetlands in the early spring, and immediately fly to the location where they nested the previous year. Each blackbird

Red-winged blackbirds can be found throughout most of North America. The male is black with red and yellow wing patches, while the female is brown.

Perching   Singing

Flying   Fighting

Figure 3   **Blackbird Behaviors**

stakes out a territory by exhibiting specific "territorial" behaviors that challenge rival males and attract females to mate and nest.

What are some of these territorial behaviors? Singing is one and exhibiting is another. To claim a territory, red-winged blackbird males fly back and forth between certain "marker spots" along the boundaries of their territories. If a male enters another male's territory, chasing and fighting occur. The males exhibit ownership by landing on high reeds and flashing their colorful shoulder patches. This behavior is referred to as "exhibiting." Some of their other behaviors are shown in Figure 3.

To observe these birds, you will need a pair of binoculars, comfortable clothing that blends in with the environment, a permanent marking pen, and your field journal.

Begin your study between dawn and 10:00 A.M. on a warm, sunny day. Birds are most active in the early morning.

Scout around the wetland for a red-winged blackbird male. (If a red-winged blackbird is hard to find, you may want to study the yellow-headed blackbird, the Brewer's blackbird, or the tricolor blackbird. All of these birds have similar behavior patterns.)

When you find a suitable bird, select a spot about 5 to 8 meters (16 to 26 ft.) from the bird. Be sure to choose a spot that allows you to see the bird's entire territory. It is important to remain as still and quiet as possible while you are watching the blackbird.

Before you begin observing the bird you have chosen, draw a map of the wetland area in your journal. Be sure to include high points such as fence posts, trees, and shrubs as well as the location of open water. When you have completed the map, begin charting the territory claimed by your bird. Watch where the bird perches, and place an "X" on the map wherever the blackbird lands. The outer X's on your map will represent the boundaries of the bird's territory. A set of twenty perch points is not uncommon for a blackbird. Label each perch point and record how often the bird lands at each one. Where does the bird perch most often?

Do you notice a slightly larger, brownish blackbird (without a shoulder patch) within the male's territory? This is the female. If the female has arrived, the point at which the male lands most often is probably the site of the nest.

It is important to notice whether or not a female is present because her presence will determine the types of behaviors the male will display. If the female is present, the male's behaviors will focus on protecting the female and the nest. After observing for a while, you may be able to predict some of the male's behaviors.

Continue to observe behavior patterns over a few days or weeks to learn how the bird's behaviors change over time. Also try to determine whether its territorial boundaries change over time. How do neighboring males behave? How does the male respond to other species of birds or mammals that enter its territory?

Whirling beetles move rapidly along the surface of slow moving water. Its special eyes allow it to hunt for prey above and below the surface simultaneously.

Animals on the Water

Walking on water may be impossible for us, but it's no problem for some animals. These animals have special adaptations and features that allow them to spend much of their time on the water's surface.

The whirling beetle spins and gyrates on top of the water. The upper and lower halves of the beetle's body are very different. Because only its bottom half is water-repellent, it swims half above and half below the surface! Even its eyes are divided into upper and lower halves. The upper half focuses on the world above the surface of the water, while the lower half functions below the water's surface.

Another animal that can be found on the water's surface is the fishing spider. Instead of spinning a web to catch its prey, this spider uses the water's surface to trap insects.

What else could you expect to see on the water? Many types of waterfowl rest and swim here. Ducks are com-

mon in wetland areas. When humans destroy wetlands, the nesting sites of many ducks and other birds are lost. Luckily, efforts to return some wildlife to these areas have met with success.

Diving ducks such as the goldeneye or common merganser usually nest in holes of old trees that border wetland areas. When wetlands are destroyed, so are these trees. If diving ducks are often present in your wetland area, you can provide them with a safe place to nest and gain some personal satisfaction by completing the following activity.

~~~~~~~~~~~~~~~~~~~~~~~~~~~~~~~~~~~~~

Diving Ducks:
How to Build a Duck Box

You can help ducks that have lost their nests by providing a place for them to build a new nest. A duck box serves the same purpose as a hole in an old tree.

Before you begin building a duck box, decide where you would like to put it. A local conservation agent can suggest the best location for the box and may be willing to help you put it up. (Diving ducks are not territorial animals, so you can put several boxes on the same pole or tree.) Also, be sure to ask the property owner for permission to place the duck box in the wetland area.

To build a duck box, you will need the following tools: a hammer, a screwdriver, a saw, and a drill. Construction materials include nails or screws, two hinges, wood (grade 3 cedar works best), and painting or staining materials.

Figure 4 shows how to construct a duck box. First, measure and cut the wood for the front, back, sides, roof, and floor of the duck box. Also, be sure to cut a hole 10 centimeters (4 in.) in diameter for the door. *Make sure an adult is present when you are cutting the wood for your duck box.* Drill five holes in the floor piece, so that any water that gets into the duck box can drain out.

Next, nail the sides and back of the box to the floor. Before nailing on the front of the duck box, attach two hinges to the back wall. After nailing on the front wall, nail the roof into the hinges. The hinges will allow you to open the top of the duck box and clean it out each spring. Remember that the

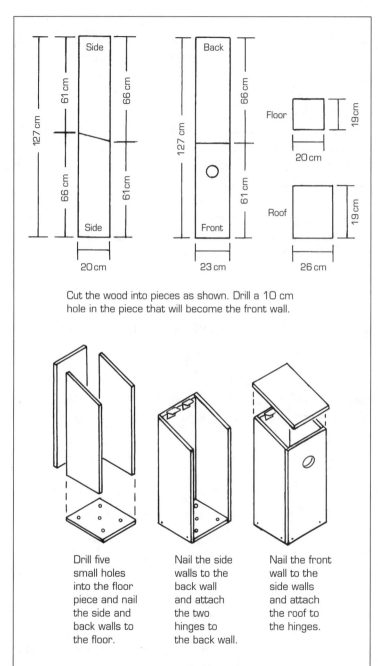

Cut the wood into pieces as shown. Drill a 10 cm hole in the piece that will become the front wall.

Drill five small holes into the floor piece and nail the side and back walls to the floor.

Nail the side walls to the back wall and attach the two hinges to the back wall.

Nail the front wall to the side walls and attach the roof to the hinges.

Figure 4 **Building a Duck Box**

roof should hang over the front wall of the duck box , so that water can flow off the roof, and not end up inside the duck box. When the duck box is complete, line the bottom with 8 centimeters (3 in.) of dry straw or sawdust.

Now all you have to do is take your duck box to a local wetland and, using large nails, attach it to a tree or strong post. To do this, lift up the roof of the duck box and drive the nails through the back wall.

Here are some hints for installing and maintaining your duck box at the wetland:

- Install the box before March 1.
- Nests should always face the water, so that young ducks can fly directly toward the water when they leave the nest.
- Nail the box to a tree or post so that it tips out and down, allowing rain to drip off.
- Each winter, clean out the box and add new straw or sawdust.

Remember that ducks must find your box before they can use it. If it is not used the year you install it, be patient. Several years may pass before ducks find your duck box and build a nest there.

Animals Under the Water

Have you ever been encouraged to go "beyond the surface" in thinking about or acting on an idea? To find out all the places where wetland animals can be found, you will surely have to go beyond the surface. You will have to go *below* the surface.

In a wetland area, the variety and abundance of living things are not limited to what you see near or on the water. The underwater environment supports an assortment of animals. Some species regularly pass back and forth between the water and air, while others spend their entire lives submerged.

You can observe creatures near the surface of the water using a bottom viewer. A collecting net will help you capture deeper-dwelling organisms. Directions for building a bottom viewer and a collecting net can be found in the Appendix at the end of this book.

The following activities will help you dive into the underwater world of the wetlands, without getting too wet!

INVESTIGATION **1**

Eye Spy:
How to Use a Bottom Viewer

Many of the organisms that dart back and forth just below the surface of the water are hard to see. When the sun reflects off the water, the glare prevents your eyes from re-creating accurate images of these creatures.

A bottom viewer is one way to catch a glimpse of these aquatic life forms. (You may also be able to use a scuba mask and snorkel if the wetland waters are not too shallow or murky for swimming.) One advantage of a bottom viewer is that you are able to see the organisms that live in the water without disturbing them. As a result, you will get a true view of what goes on below the surface.

You may also want to take a collecting jar or sampling pan (see Appendix), a magnifying lens, wading boots, and a safety vest. As always, your journal will come in handy.

A bottom viewer maximizes light's penetration of the water, especially on a sunny day. First, select a site where you can easily reach the water's edge. Place your bottom viewer a little below the water's surface and look directly down, through the transparent film. It may take your eyes a few moments to focus. When your eyes have adjusted, start noting the different types of organisms that you see. Focus on their

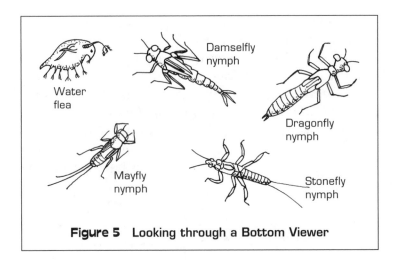

Water flea

Damselfly nymph

Dragonfly nymph

Mayfly nymph

Stonefly nymph

Figure 5 Looking through a Bottom Viewer

shapes and movements. Then, record or draw what you see in your journal. Some of the creatures will exhibit the most intriguing behaviors and appearances. You will probably see many unfamiliar organisms. Using a field guide to help you, try to identify them.

What can you expect to see with a bottom viewer? You may see a variety of insects, amphibians, worms, fishes, and crustaceans. You may even see a predatory diving beetle making its way to the surface to breathe. Tadpoles generally cruise the bottom, feeding on algae that grows on the surface of plants or rocks.

You will probably see water fleas, small crustaceans about the size of a pinhead. See Figure 5. Like their relatives—shrimp, crayfish, and lobster—water fleas have two pairs of antennae. Their jerky swimming style makes them easy to recognize. Water fleas are important in the wetlands because they are the primary source of food for many fishes and insects.

As you continue to view the underwater world, you may see small fish, tadpoles, or frogs. You may also see the nymphs (the immature stage) of damselflies, dragonflies, mayflies, and stone flies. The nymphs of the dragonflies are predators that wait silently in the weeds for prey. Snails, cray-fish, and aquatic worms may also be abundant.

A Riveting Event: From Tadpole to Frog

Do you look the same as you did the day you were born? Of course not. Even though you have changed a great deal over the years, some of your features—the shape of your nose and the color of your eyes—have not changed much. Unlike humans, some species look very different at stages of their lives. Sometimes a complete transformation takes place.

You can witness this type of change, or **metamorphosis**, in **amphibians**. Although frogs and their young are the most common amphibians in wetlands, you may also find salamanders, toads, and mud puppies. All these amphibians lay their eggs in wetland areas.

Capturing adult frogs takes practice and stealth. They hide along the edge of the water. When they see a human approaching, they leap into the water and swim away. You will probably have better luck catching tadpoles. You may encounter tadpoles of a leopard frog, a wood frog, a tree frog, and a bull frog. You may also be able to capture a toad's young.

An adult frog differs from a tadpole in both appearance and behavior. The adult is a predator that eats insects and small fish, while the tadpole is a vegetarian that scrapes algae and scum from rocks and plant surfaces. The adult frog breathes air through lungs. The tadpole breathes primarily through gills. A tadpole lacks legs and looks much like a fish. The life cycle of a frog is shown in Figure 6 on the next page.

The time it takes to complete this amazing metamorpho-sis varies from species to species. Some tadpoles metamor-

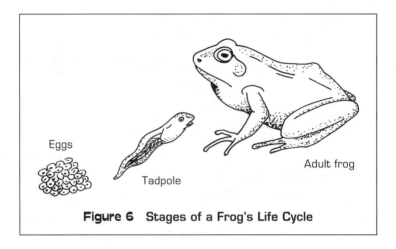

Figure 6 **Stages of a Frog's Life Cycle**

phosize in just a few weeks; others take more than a year. The bull frog, the largest frog, requires two full winters to complete its transformation. Are you ready to witness some of the fascinating changes that occur in frogs? Here's how you can observe and monitor the changes.

First, look for frog eggs—jellylike masses with white circular eggs suspended inside. Less than a tablespoon of this substance, can produce many young frogs. Although female frogs lay thousands of eggs, only a few make it to maturity. Most are eaten by other animals. If you observe them with a hand lens, you should be able to see the embryo growing inside the egg. The young tadpoles will soon emerge. Do not collect these eggs. Leave them to hatch.

Next, choose a shallow area along the water's edge and carefully watch for movement in the water. When you have spotted the tadpoles, collect five to ten with your collecting net (see Appendix). Place the tadpoles in a large container—such as an empty peanut butter jar—that has been filled with wetlands water (tap water is not a natural environment for tadpoles). Also pick up some submerged leaves, sticks, or rocks—the algae on them will provide food for the growing tadpoles.

Bring the tadpoles home and raise them in a shallow dishpan or aquarium. (You do not need an aerator or air pump.) The type of water in your observation tank is important. If you have to add tap water to the original wetland water, let it sit for 2 to 3 days before adding it to the wetland water. During this time, any chlorine in the water will settle out. (Chlorine is generally added to a city's water-treatment process. It acts as a disinfectant, and could kill the tadpoles.) Also make sure that the water is not hot. Hot water contains less oxygen, and will **asphyxiate** the growing tadpoles. Tadpoles breathe through gills, but they can take in oxygen by gulping air and holding it in their mouth. Also, try to store the observation tank in a cool area.

Be sure to observe the tadpoles every day, and record any changes in your journal. Note their movements and measure their growth. Indicate where and how they feed and note any interaction among individuals. Which legs appear first? When do they appear? How much time elapsed between the appearance of the first pair of legs and the second pair? You may also want to make drawings of your observations. There is so much to see in this remarkable metamorphosis.

Underwater Insects: How Clean Is Your Wetland?

Aquatic organisms can tell you a great deal about water quality. For example, some species, such as stone flies, cannot tolerate polluted water. Therefore, their presence indicates that a body of water is clean and well oxygenated. Bloodworms or midge larvae have a great tolerance for polluted water, so their presence indicates poor water quality.

Water quality often varies from season to season. A body of water that may be able to support species that indicate high water quality in the spring, may not be able to support them in late summer because warm water cannot hold as much oxygen as cold water.

To collect **indicator organisms** and determine the quality of your water, you will need a collecting net, a sampling pan to sort organisms for identification, several bowls, forceps, and a field guide. (Instructions for constructing a collecting net and sampling pan are given in the Appendix.) A state conservation organization can tell you where to find a simple picture key of **aquatic** organisms. You can use this key to classify the organisms you find. You may also contact the Isaak Walton League in Arlington, Virginia, and request the general procedures and keys they have developed for identifying stream and water critters.

When you have organized all of your equipment, locate a wetland area where you can collect aquatic organisms. Aquatic creatures need oxygen, so they will congregate in rocky areas. Choose an area where water is moving over stones and other objects. This area will have the highest concentration of oxygen. (If you cannot find a rocky area, choose an area that is easily accessible.)

If the oxygen level is high and no chemicals or excess soils are present, many kinds of organisms can be found. The greater the variety of organisms, the better the water quality. Other things affecting the number and kind of creatures in a wetland include the depth, velocity, and temperature of the water.

To take a sample, drag the collecting net over the bottom of the water and pick up everything the net will hold. Remove rocks, sticks, and leaf litter from the water so that you can observe the small organisms among them. When the net becomes heavy with materials, empty the contents into a sampling pan.

Next, fill one of the bowls with water from the site and sort through the materials you have found. When you find small organisms, use forceps to transfer them to the bowl of water. As the surface of the material you collected dries out, some of the animals will attempt to move toward the bottom of the sampling pan.

Table 2 Tolerance of Aquatic Species to Pollution

Intolerant	Moderately Intolerant	Fairly Tolerant	Very Tolerant
Stone fly larva	Riffle beetle larva	Leech	Aquatic worm
Alder fly larva	Damselfly larva	Black fly larva	Left-handed
Dobsonfly larva	Dragonfly larva	Turbellaria	snail
Water penny adult	Biting midge larva	Right-handed	Blood worm
and larva	Mayfly larva	snail	midge larva
Damselfly larva	Crayfish	Sowbug	
Caddisfly larva	Mussels	Midge larva	
Scud	Clam		
Crane fly larva			

Take samples from as many different parts of the water environment as possible. For example, if you are taking samples from a stream, collect materials alongside the bank and from the deepest part of the stream. Also search for organisms underneath and among masses of brown waterlogged leaves. You may find interesting organisms on floating and submerged wood. Collect all living things, even worms and mussels. They all indicate the kind of water found in the wetland.

When you have collected enough organisms, try to identify them. If the wetland water is clean, most of the organisms that you find should be moderately tolerant or intolerant of pollution.

Depending on the time of year, wetlands will have aquatic organisms from two or three of the categories listed in Table 2. Your state has probably developed procedures to give your water a numerical value for water quality. If not, you can obtain this information from the Isaak Walton League. Illinois, Indiana, Missouri, Alabama, Arkansas, Georgia, Colorado, and many other states have volunteer stream-monitoring programs with which you can become involved.

CHAPTER 2

Rambling Through Roots, Reeds, and Rushes

WETLAND PLANTS ARE KNOWN AS **hydrophytes**, which means "water loving." They have have unique adaptations that help them thrive in water-saturated environments.

As you begin to investigate wetland plants, you may notice that some grow in areas where the water is shallow, while others are always found in deeper water.

Wetland plants can be classified by where their roots and stems are in relation to the surface of the water. See Figure 7. The roots, stems, and leaves of **submerged plants** such as pondweeds are all underwater. **Emergent plants** rise above the surface of the water. Although the roots of cattails, arrowhead, and bulrush grow in wet soil for all or part of the year, their stems and leaves stand well above the surface of the water.

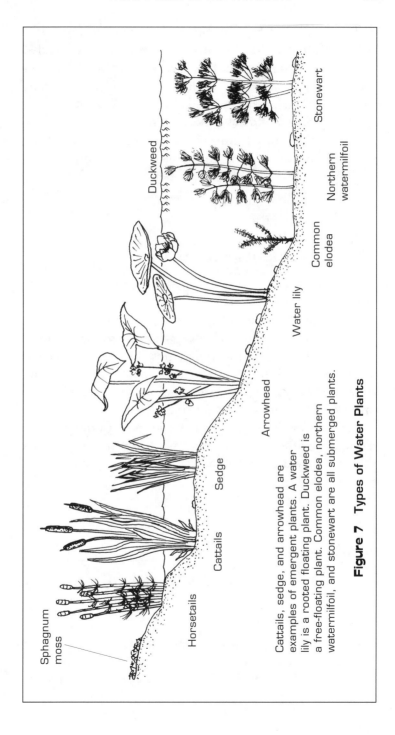

Sphagnum moss

Horsetails

Cattails

Sedge

Arrowhead

Water lily

Duckweed

Common elodea

Northern watermilfoil

Stonewart

Cattails, sedge, and arrowhead are examples of emergent plants. A water lily is a rooted floating plant. Duckweed is a free-floating plant. Common elodea, northern watermilfoil, and stonewart are all submerged plants.

Figure 7 Types of Water Plants

There are two types of floating plants. **Rooted float-ing plants** have root systems that are firmly embedded into the ground beneath the water. Water lilies, for example, send up broad leaves to the water's surface, but their roots extend deep below the surface. Other floating plants, known as as **free-floating plants**, are not attached to the bottom at all. One common example is duckweed, which generally occurs in large numbers because it reproduces rapidly. Duckweed roots dangle below the surface of the water as the plants drift with the water's motion. Duck-weed is a beneficial plant because it filters out pollutants.

Plants Near the Water

In the Introduction, you learned about the different types of wetlands. Each type of wetland supports different plants. For example, swamps generally have woody plants such as trees and shrubs, whereas grasses, rushes, sedges, and cattails grow in marshes. Spongy plants such as mosses are abundant in bogs. Because bogs are sometimes remnants of much larger swamps or wetlands, they often support rare or endangered plants.

The plants in a wetland have adapted to the specific demands of their environments. As you observe plants that flourish at the water's edge, note the structures and features that have made each plant a successful inhabitant of that environment.

ʃʃʃʃʃʃʃʃʃʃʃʃʃʃʃ

INVESTIGATION 4

How to Conduct a Botanical Line Transect

Like animals, certain plants are generally found closer to the water's edge than others. You can learn about the changes and transitions that occur at various distances from the water by conducting an inventory of an area along a straight path.

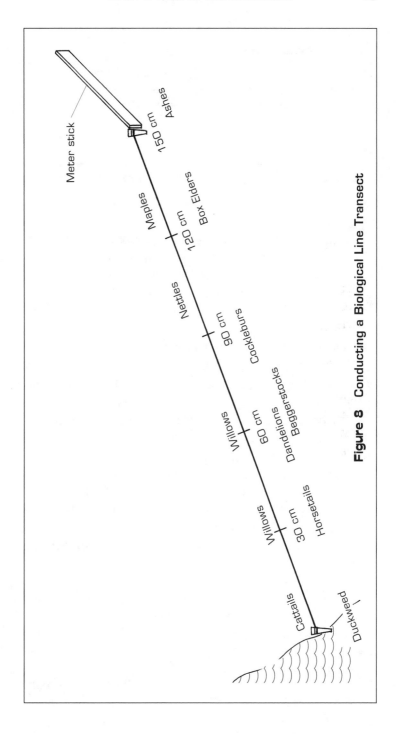

Figure 8 Conducting a Biological Line Transect

Table 3 Plants Along a Line Transect		
Interval	Name of Plant	Description
1 m	Duckweed	Washed up on the shore
2 m		
3 m		
4 m		

This type of survey, known as a **line transect**, is particularly good for observing **successional** changes—changes that occur as you follow the line farther from the water.

To make a line transect, you will need 20 to 30 meters (65 to 100 ft.) of strong cord or string that has been marked at 1-meter (3-ft.) intervals, a meter stick, a measuring tape, plant-identification books, and your journal.

First, select a site. Walk along the shore of that site with a meter stick in your hand. Close your eyes, turn around two or three times, and toss the meter stick away from the water. Lay the string from the point at which you are standing (at the water's edge) to the spot where the zero point on the meter stick has landed. See Figure 8.

Observe the vegetation growing within 50 centimeters (20 in.) of each side of the string. In your journal, record what you see at 1-meter (3-ft.) intervals. Be sure to include the location and date of your observations. You may want to draw plants that you cannot identify, and make a summary table like the one shown in Table 3 to help organize the information you collect.

Be sure to note any vegetation patterns as well as any changes in soil conditions or water levels. Are plants closer to the shore shorter or taller than plants farther away from the water's edge? Do you notice differences in the color or shape of leaves?

Weighing In: How to Determine the Water Content of Plants

What happens when you bite into a piece of watermelon or a slice of orange? These fruits release large quantities of juice because they contain a great deal of water. Most living things are composed of water; your body is approximately 70 percent water.

Most water plants are **herbaceous** and have soft succulent tissues that contain large quantities of water. Land plants usually congregate in wet, moist places. Plants that live in dry habitats, such as deserts, have evolved ways to store water in their tissues and roots.

In this investigation you will collect plants from different parts of a wetland and compare their water content. You should notice that truly aquatic plants such as duckweed, milfoil, and elodea contain larger quantities of water than do cattails, rushes, and reeds. Do you think trees and shrubs contain more or less water than duckweed? Do they contain more or less water than cattails?

Begin by gathering collecting bags, scissors or tree-trimming shears, a balance, masking tape, a permanent marking pen, a cookie sheet, and your journal.

Using the knowledge you gained from your other experiences in the wetlands, identify and collect plant species that represent the various habitats of the wetland. Choose plants from different places along the line transect discussed in Investigation 4. You will need two or three specimens of each plant. To make sure that the plants do not lose any moisture, keep the samples wet, out of the sun, and in a plastic bag.

Bring the plants home, and rinse each one in a sink to remove mud or other nonplant material. Using a small piece of masking tape and the permanent marking pen, label each plant (Specimen 1, Specimen 2, Specimen 3, etc.). Place each plant on the balance and record its mass in your jour-

Table 4   Water Content Analysis

Plant Species	Habitat	Wet Mass	Dry Mass	Water Content
1. Cattail	Near water	125 g	65 g	60 g
2.				
3.				
4.				
5.				
6.				
7.				

nal. You may have to bend or break the plant's roots, stems, and leaves, so that the entire plant will fit on the balance. If you break the plants, however, the water in their tissues will escape faster. Place several unweighed samples of each plant aside to test for water loss.

Next, place the plants on a cookie sheet and then into an oven that has been preheated to 95°C (200°F). Heat the plants for about 10 minutes—until the leaves can be crumbled and the plant stems snapped. Keep checking the plants to make sure they do not burn. *Ask an adult for assistance with this step.*

Measure the dried mass of each plant and record that data in a table like the one shown in Table 4. Subtract the dry mass from the wet mass to determine the water content of each plant. Is a plant's water content related to its habitat?

PROJECT 5

Soil Saver: Planting a Willow Tree

If you walk along the edge of a wetland stream you will probably discover spots with no plants. The absence of plants may be the result of periodic flooding or overgrazing by livestock. Without plant cover, the soil is likely to erode into the stream.

Farmers and ranchers are being asked to limit animal access to streams so that the surrounding land will not erode. You can help limit erosion, too. Planting a few willow trees along the banks of a stream can help the stream heal itself.

Why willows? These trees have a unique ability. If you cut a branch from a living willow tree and place it in the ground, roots will sprout and a new tree will grow. Willows are also the ideal choice for protecting a stream bank because clumps of willows share a single, strong root system.

Before planting new trees, ask a local ranger or conservation agent for assistance and obtain the permission of the land owner. You will need tree-trimming tools for cutting willow branches and a metal pole (a rebar used in construction works well) to make holes in the soil along the stream bank. You may want to bring along a camera to make a visual record of your efforts. Your journal will also be useful.

Where do you begin? First find a spot along a stream where the soil is exposed and erosion is obvious. With your tree-trimming tools, cut thumb-sized branches from a willow tree. (Do not remove the leaves from the branches.) Using the metal pole, make holes about 30 centimeters (12 in.) apart in the soil. Each hole should be deep enough to prevent the willow branch from washing into the stream when the water level rises.

Place the freshly cut end of each willow branch into one of the holes. Press the soil around the branch and pack it down by stepping firmly around the branch. Plant a few extras because some of the branches will not sprout. Return to the site a few weeks later to see how many of the branches have begun to develop into new trees.

✔ Doing More

You may also want to plant wetland species that have died out due to human activity or changes in environmental conditions. A local conservation agent can suggest which plant species would be most beneficial to a particular wetland area.

The willow tree is found in almost every type of wetland. It prevents erosion and is a source of food for many animals.

Some of the species you may want to add to a wetland include cattails, arrowroot, reeds, and water purslane. Be sure not to introduce any **exotic plant species** into a wetland. These plants will compete with native species for light, water, and soil nutrients. Purple loosestrife, water hyacinth, pampas grass, and Asiatic milfoil are all examples of exotic plants. You should remove these plants, not plant more.

Be sure to plant species that are free of animal pests, and never bring in plants from an area that has been invaded by pests. The zebra mussel is a particularly troublesome in-

vader. It attaches itself to aquatic plants and is sometimes brought from one lake to another by boats. You can avoid this problem by only moving plants within the same wetland.

Plants in the Water

L ife in the water requires a unique set of adaptations. Many aquatic plants lack the tough supporting tissues that land plants have. Their thin tissue layers enable them to absorb oxygen, carbon dioxide, and mineral salts from the water. Some aquatic plants have roots that serve as anchors and take up nutrients from the water bottom. While most aquatic plants have air pockets within their tissues, floating leaves have exceptionally large air pockets to help maintain **buoyancy**.

The activities in this section will set you afloat on an aquatic adventure that will allow you to explore the adaptations and diversity of submerged, emergent, and floating plants.

PROJECT **6**

A Pressing Matter: How to Collect and Save Aquatic Plants

Have you ever kept a photo album? These photographs are visual reminders of vacations, celebrations, and other special events. You can create an "album" of your favorite wetland plants, too.

Begin this project by collecting some of the plants you would like to remember. You will need a large plastic bag and scissors or a handheld tree-trimming tool. Choose plants that are abundant and collect only one sample of each species. Try to select plants that are representative of the types of plants growing in a particular area.

It is important to make sure that your plants do not dry

out. After you have collected the plants, fill the plastic bag with water. Shake it thoroughly, and then pour the excess water out. Then, tie the top of the plastic bag closed so that the plants will stay moist.

Bring the plants back to the shade of your house, and gather the following equipment: newspapers, paper towels or a bath towel, and plywood or heavy cardboard. Place the plants on a piece of paper towel or bath towel, and blot both sides of the plants to remove excess water. Lay each dried plant on a separate sheet of newspaper, making sure it is flat and all the leaves are spread apart.

Fold the newspaper over the plant and place several sheets of newspaper on top of the one containing the plant. These additional sheets will **wick**, removing any remaining water from the plant's tissues. If all of the water does not evaporate, the plant could rot.

Next, place another plant in a new "newspaper sandwich" and layer additional sheets of newspaper on top. When all the plants have been placed between sheets of newspaper, lay a piece of cardboard or plywood on top of the stack and another piece under it. Tie the stack with a rope or place a heavy object on top of the pile to compress it. Put the collection in an airy place that does not receive direct sunlight. If your collection is large, you may want to make two stacks. Pressing and drying may take up to 3 weeks, depending on humidity. Smaller plants and those with thin stems will dry first. When they are dry, mount the plants on white paper. Write the plant's name below the specimen with a permanent marking pen.

Many university science or botany departments keep a plant collection in an area called a **herbarium**. You may be able to add your collection to theirs. Contact the people who organize the collection and ask them how they would like you to mount and label your specimens. They will probably want to know where and when you located the plants as well as the plants' common and scientific names. These professionals should be able to help you identify the plants.

Growing and Floating:
How to Monitor Duckweed Growth

Have you noticed that water in some wetland areas is covered with a blanket of green? If you look closely, you will see that this covering is actually a plant—probably duckweed.

Duckweed is generally a small plant—one variety is just 2 millimeters ($^7/_{100}$ in.) long. It has tiny leaves with rootlets that hang down into the water. The tiny roots serve as a home for algae and other microscopic animals. Because duckweed is a floating plant, its location is determined by the wind and water currents.

When conditions are right, duckweed can reproduce at a phenomenal rate. How is this possible? To begin with, duckweed can reproduce in two different ways—sexually and by **budding**. Sometimes in late spring or early summer, duckweed grows so quickly that it forms a mat dense enough to support the weight of a red-winged blackbird.

Duckweed growth is often enhanced by fertilizers that wash in from surrounding agricultural areas. When fertilizer runoff is excessive, lakes clog up with duckweed and other aquatic plants. If the population of duckweed grows too quickly, the plants will begin to die, giving off a putrid smell that may cause an entire wetland area to stink.

Monitoring the growth patterns of duckweed can be very interesting. If you would like to spend some time with a fast-growing population and one of the world's smallest flowering plants, then this investigation is for you.

*Duckweed is one of the world's
smallest flowering plants. It
grows rapidly on the surface
of many wetlands.*

Begin by gathering duckweed with a kitchen strainer and a large container or bucket. Place 80 to 100 duckweed plants in your collecting bucket and then fill it with wetland water.

After returning home, gather 6 to 12 clear drinking glasses, lawn or garden fertilizer, an old set of measuring spoons, a permanent marking pen, a strong light source, and your journal.

If drinking glasses are not available, you can use 2-liter soda bottles instead. Cut the top off each soda bottle and fill the bottom with water. Number the bottles 1a, 1b, 2a, 2b, 3a, and 3b with the permanent marking pen. If more than six bottles are available, continue to number the bottles in the same way.

Add $1/8$ teaspoon of fertilizer to bottles 1a and 1b, $1/4$ teaspoon to bottles 2a and 2b, and $1/2$ teaspoon to bottles 3a and 3b. If you have more than six bottles, continue to add greater amounts of fertilizer to each set of bottles. Keep track of how much fertilizer you have added to each bottle in your field journal. Also note the date, time, and appearance of what is in each bottle.

Why should you add the same amount of fertilizer to two bottles? Repeating experiments is very important in science. If your findings for bottle 1a and 1b are the same, the results are reliable. If the results are different, something went wrong and you should repeat the experiment. Note the amount of fertilizer added on the side of the container.

Next, stir the fertilizer in each bottle until it has completely dissolved. Add ten healthy duckweed plants to each container. Make sure that the plants are not about to bud.

Observe the bottles daily and record any changes in your journal. What impact does the fertilizer have on your duckweed populations? How does the concentration of fertilizer affect the population? What effect does the fertilizer have on the algae that you inadvertently introduced into the water along with the duckweed?

You may be able to borrow a kit that can measure the concentration of nitrates and phosphates—two ingredients in fertilizer—in water from a conservation agent or a science teacher. If so, test the water in your wetland area to see how much fertilizer is being released into the wetland.

✔ Doing More

Algae are so small that they break loose in the water and float freely. Algae are even carried in the air when dried particles on branches or soil are picked up by the wind. Given enough time, algae will colonize almost any location.

Observing the variety of algae from a wetland can reveal a great deal about the quality of its water. Using a microscope to view your algae collections can lead to many interesting findings. Algae can be scraped from almost any

In wetland environments, algae are a major source of food and oxygen.

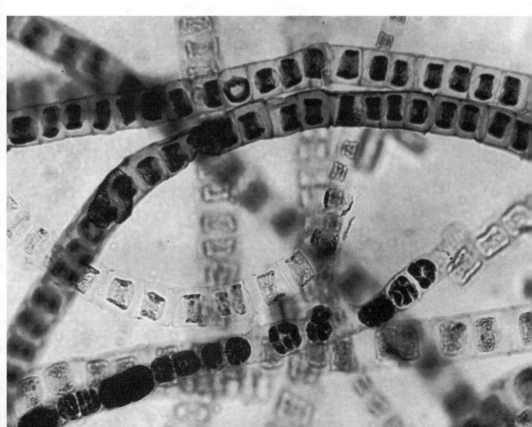

surface in a wetland area, placed on a microscope slide, and observed. You can also collect algae using the algae sampler described in the Appendix.

A Temporary Change of Address: How to Make a Plant Aquarium

If you would like to monitor the growth of wetland plants for a longer period of time, build a plant aquarium. You will need a large glass container that has been rinsed to remove any soap residue. Soap is not hard on plants but it will kill any animals that you might add.

First, cover the bottom of the container with a layer of gravel and small rocks. Cover this layer with a 2- to 3-centimeter (1-in.) layer of sand. If possible, collect the sand, rocks, and gravel from the wetland site, too. Fill the container with water from the wetland and let it sit for a few days in a spot that gets some sun, but is not in direct sunlight.

Now you are ready to begin adding plants. Begin by adding just two or three different types of floating and emergent plants. After about a week, you may want to add a few small animals such as fish or macroinvertebrates from the wetland. Don't add too many because wild water animals are hard to keep. (It may be better to keep them in a smaller jar, observe them for a few days, and then return them to the wetland.)

Continue to monitor your aquarium every day and note any changes in your journal.

CHAPTER 3

Noticing Networks: Interactions and Relationships

TO LIVE A BALANCED HEALTHY LIFE, people depend on the services and input of others. The plants and animals in a wetland also function together in a supportive system. They provide each other with basic needs—food, water, oxygen, carbon dioxide, and shelter. Because a wetland contains a diversity of life-forms, there is a wide variety of relationships and interactions between the organisms. Populations interact with each other and are affected by each other.

Many different types of animals are attracted to a wetland because the wetland contains many different types of plants. These plants provide the animals with food and shelter. Many types of plants can survive in a wetland because the wetland

59

supports a variety of animals that pollinate flowers and disperse seeds.

Interactions between organisms also affect the environment. In addition, the environmental conditions of the wetland and the number and quality of its populations are influenced by human actions.

Are these associations helpful or harmful? How can we influence the patterns and processes that occur in wetlands? The following investigations will help you examine the established and dynamic networks of wetlands.

Feeding and Cooperative Relationships

Organisms have established many kinds of relationships so that they can live and thrive in wetland areas. Doing the following activities will help you understand how organisms interact with each other.

INVESTIGATION 7

Marsh Menus: How to Observe Food Chains

Can you imagine a day without food? Food provides you with the energy you need to carry out daily activities. Energy flows through an ecosystem in **food chains** and **food webs**. A food chain outlines how energy derived from food is carried from one organism to another.

Every food chain starts with the sun, which provides plants with the energy they need to grow and carry out photosynthesis. When that plant is eaten by an animal, the energy from the sun is transferred to the animal. When one animal eats another, the energy is transferred from the prey to the predator.

Look at the food chain shown in Figure 9. The sun provides all the energy the algae need to grow and reproduce.

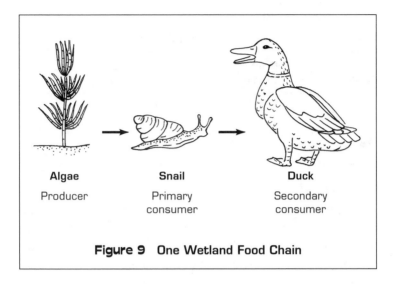

Algae   **Snail**   **Duck**

Producer   Primary   Secondary
                  consumer   consumer

Figure 9   One Wetland Food Chain

The algae are eaten by snails, and the snails in turn are eaten by ducks. The energy from the sun is transferred to the algae and then to the snail and finally to the duck. Food webs are a bit more complex. They outline how different food chains combine to form a network of feeding relationships.

To get a glimpse of some of the feeding relationships that abound in wetland areas, try to identify as many food chains as possible. Remember that all food chains begin with the sun. The sun's energy is absorbed by a plant, which is called a **producer**. Plants are considered producers because they can fuel their own growth. **Primary consumers** such as snails are animals that feed directly on plants. **Secondary consumers** such as ducks are animals that eat primary consumers. In other words, they are meat-eaters. Can you figure out what type of consumer you are?

For this exploration you will need your journal, field guides, and keen observation skills. First, find an area where you can sit and observe. Begin by focusing on one animal, such as an insect, bird, or frog. Record the animal's eating behaviors in your journal. Describe what it eats and how much time it spends searching for food. Select other animals and note their feeding behaviors.

Table 5   Wetland Feeding Relationships

Producers	Primary Consumers	Secondary Consumers
Algae	Snails	Ducks

When you have observed a number of organisms, you can begin to make a chart like the one shown in Table 5. In your chart, record the name or description of the producer, primary consumer, and secondary consumer (if sighted). Make additional observations on the frequency of the feeding and if the animal eats more than one type of producer.

Turning over a New Leaf: How to Observe Cycles

Have you noticed any changes in yourself? Your neighborhood? Your school? Do these changes occur quickly or do they take place gradually? A tremendous amount of change takes place in wetland areas. Some of these changes occur rapidly, while others require days, weeks, or months. Many of the changes are cyclic in nature. For example, the productivity of a wetland is tied into the cycle of life, death, decay, and rebirth.

Cattails, willows, rushes, algae, duckweed, and a multitude of other water plants sprout and grow each spring. All of this material, called **biomass**, eventually ends up at the bottom of the wetland. Over time, layers of the decayed remains of plants and animals build up in a wetland. Over many,

many years, a wetland may develop into a wet prairie meadow. This change occurs so slowly that it is difficult to detect. The following investigation will allow you to see the process over a much shorter period of time.

Begin by locating a site at the water's edge or in a wet lowland area. Using a garden trowel, turn over a fresh layer of earth and look for the remains of last year's growth. You may come across portions of twigs, seeds, or stems. If you continue digging, you will notice that the soil periodically changes color. Each new color may indicate a new year. Note this layering in your journal.

Next, search for leaves of common wetland plants. Select some that are green and others that have dried or become brown. Note the condition of each leaf in your journal along with the date.

Dig a deep hole in a wetland area and place several leaves at the bottom. Cover these leaves with a few centimeters of the soil you removed from the hole. Place several more leaves on top of the new soil layer and cover them with soil too. Repeat this procedure until you have filled in the hole. You can also place some leaves at the surface. Mark the spot carefully with a stick.

Dig five or six additional holes and layer them with leaves and soil, too. Also mark the location of these holes with a stick. In your journal, make a map to show the location of the holes.

Return to the site you have marked 2 weeks later. Carefully dig into the layers and examine the leaves. Have they begun to decay? Refill the hole and keep returning to the sites every 2 weeks to check on the condition of the leaves. Did the leaves that were placed deeper in the ground decay faster than those placed closer to the surface? Be sure to note your observations in your journal.

Oxygen is the key to good decomposition and decay. When the oxygen source is gone, or not available to bacteria, it takes longer for leaves to decay. In the wet environment of the marshland, the water may prevent oxygen from moving into the soil. An oxygen-deficient area contains mostly

anaerobic bacteria. You can tell when an area contains many anaerobic bacteria because it smells of sulfur, which has an odor similar to rotten eggs.

✔ Doing More

Start a compost pile in your yard. Also make a compost pile in the wetland and leave it for a month or more. Return and go through the pile carefully. See what kinds of animals have invaded the pile. Does the action in the compost pile accelerate when the pile is periodically mixed?

Up a Tree: How to Recognize Symbiotic Relationships

Do you have friends that you can really rely on? Will they support you when you need them? This type of relationship is not unique among humans. In wetland areas, a tree is a haven for a multitude of small animals who rely on it as a home. Many small plants also grow on trees. A relationship in which one or more organisms live together is called **symbiosis**. A tree and its inhabitants may have a symbiotic relationship. In some symbiotic relationships, only one of the organisms benefits. In others, both organisms benefit.

In this activity, you can sharpen your investigative skills by searching for evidence of symbiotic relationships in a local wetland area. Most symbiotic relationships involve providing food or offering shelter. Here are some examples:

Galls form when an insect, fungus, or bacteria enters a plant, causing an irritation. The plant responds by developing tissue that forms a protective layer to isolate the irritant.

- A willow tree provides nesting materials for birds. As birds carry twigs and leaves through the wetland, they disperse willow seeds attached to the nesting materials.
- As beavers build their homes, they transport tree branches from one place to another. Depending on where the beavers deposit any willow branches that they pick up, the limbs may develop into new trees.
- The population of lichens and mosses growing on the bark of trees is controlled by the beetles that eat them.

Before you begin to look for other symbiotic relationships, gather the following materials: an insect sweep net (see Appendix), field guides, magnifying lens, and your journal.

First, select a large tree and describe it in your journal. What species is it? How tall is it? What is its girth? Do its branches grow close to the ground? How long are the branches? What do the leaves look like? You may also want to make a drawing of the tree.

Now begin to look for large animals, nests, and hives in and around the tree. List these in your journal. Look for insects by running the sweep net over the surface of the tree's leaves.

Examine the tree for **galls**. A gall is a swelling of plant tissue induced by the presence of insect parasites. Galls on a willow tree may indicate the presence of eggs laid by a female wasp.

You may also see lichens and mosses on the bark. Ferns can sometimes be found on branches. In the southeastern United States, Spanish moss hangs from the branches of wetland trees. In older trees, mushrooms and their relatives often grow from tree trunks. What types of plants, lichens, or fungi are growing on the tree that you selected?

The final step of your investigation is to determine how plants living under the tree are related to the tree. Which organisms benefit the tree? How do they improve the trees ability to survive?

✔ Doing More

Study a tree in your yard or near your school. Compare the results with the wetland tree.

Hiding Places: How to Find Protective Relationships

Have you ever looked and looked for something, and finally found it right where you looked the first time? Somehow, it blended in with its surroundings.

In wetland environments, the water can provide a safe place for animals to hide. You might catch some of these animals if you pull up a water-soaked board, an old tire, a discarded bottle, or a water-logged tree limb. You could also grab live roots, grasses, or stems; or dig down into dead leaves and twigs. You will find living creatures in all of these places.

To uncover the many hiding places within a wetland, you will need your journal; a flat, wide plywood board; and animal identification books. Select five to ten spots that might harbor a variety of underwater animals.

Begin by placing the plywood board near the water. Pull out a handful of dead wet leaves and lay them on the board. When the leaves are exposed to sunlight, the water creatures will wriggle about hoping to fall back into the water. Note in your journal the kind and number of animals found in this environment.

Explore other wetland locations in the same way. For each site, record the number and kinds of animals as well as any similarities between species. You should find some variation in the types of animals at different locations.

One factor that determines whether a creature lives in a particular body of water is the oxygen content of the water.

Moving streams have higher concentrations of oxygen than the stagnant ponds of a swamp.

One exception to this rule is a pond that has green algae and various floating pond plants. On a sunny day, the plants can produce enough oxygen to support a fair-sized population of aquatic animals. Other environmental factors that affect underwater animal populations include the water's *pH* (degree of acidity) and concentration of chemical pollutants.

Making a list—or collection—of the animals living in various parts of a wetland area will help you determine the health of its waters. Healthy water has many different types of animals. Poor water has fewer species and, in most cases, one or two species are dominant.

✔ Doing More

Another place to look for animals is inside the tissues of wetland plants. You will need a knife to examine living plant tissue.

Begin by checking the plant stems and leaves for abnormal spots. These spots may be bruises caused by large animals, but they could also contain insect larvae. Carefully cut away the tissue to see what is underneath the spot. ***Do not cut your fingers.***

Interactions and Indicators of Health

Ecosystems are always in flux. If any of the system is disturbed, other parts will also be disturbed. Nevertheless, nature is usually able to maintain a healthy balance within an established environment.

How can we detect disturbances early? We can look for organisms that give us a signal that all is fine or that the health of the ecosystem has deteriorated. The following activities allow you to use organisms and conditions to indicate the quality of the air and water in a local wetland area.

"Lichen" It More and More: How to Assess Air Quality

Why is it that some organisms just can't be found in a particular area? The environment may contain either too little or too much of a substance that affects the organism. As you learned in Chapter 1, organisms that are very sensitive and can survive only under certain chemical and physical conditions are known as indicator species. For example, the presence of lichens indicates good air quality.

What is a lichen? A lichen is an organism that consists of a fungus and an alga living in a cooperative symbiotic relationship. The alga produces sugar for the fungus, and the fungus absorbs nutrients from the air. The fungus also helps keep in moisture and anchors the lichen to a tree or rock. Lichens grow in habitats where neither the alga nor the fungus could live alone.

Lichens remove a variety of compounds from the air and concentrate them in their tissues. If the air in their environment contains pollutants, such as sulfur dioxide or other sulfur compounds, these materials build up in the lichens' tissues. Eventually, the concentration of pollutants becomes so great that the lichens die.

In this investigation, you will be on the prowl for lichens. If at least one-quarter of the dominant trees in your wetland have lichens covering more than one-eighth of their surface area, you know that the air quality in the area is good.

To complete this assessment, you will need your journal, a plastic bag, a magnifying lens, and a measuring tape.

Begin by observing the dominant trees in your wetland area for the presence of lichens. The fungus part is usually white, but is sometimes orange. It consists of woven tubes. The alga part is usually green or blue-green and is embedded in the fungal tubes. Record the approximate percentage of trees in the area that have lichens on their trunks or branches.

How clean is the air in a particular wetland or wooded area? The presence of lichens indicates that air quality is good.

Remove a small sample of any kind of lichen that you see more than once and look at it closely with a magnifying lens. As you collect each sample, place it in a plastic bag, record the location, and estimate how much of the tree is covered by lichens. When you have collected a number of samples, any differences between the lichens should be more obvious. Also, look for lichens on rocks.

Using the data you have recorded in your journal, try to make some generalizations about the condition of air quality in your wetland area.

INVESTIGATION 12

Wetland Health:
How to Assess Water Quality

How healthy is your wetland? Are there warning signs that can give you a hint of its condition? There are a number of ways to determine the overall health of a wetland. Just as a medical doctor has a list of items to examine during your general checkup, there is a list you can use to evaluate the general health of a wetland.

Natural wetlands go through constant change. As a result, the water clarity and cleanliness are subject to change. For example, during the hot days of late summer, the water heats up and loses large quantities of oxygen. In addition, water levels may be lower than normal due to natural evaporation or lack of rain.

Because the condition of a wetland is subject to such seasonal changes, you must monitor a wetland for several months or even an entire year to determine its overall health. You must consider the water's appearance, amount of vegetative cover, types of aquatic life, nearby land use and structures, and amount of litter.

To conduct a checkup of a wetland area, make a few photocopies of the data sheet shown on the next page. (Figure 10) Take the copies to the wetland you wish to evaluate and fill them out. You may want to use separate data sheets for running-water sites and still-water sites. After completing your data sheets, rate the overall health of the wetland area. Can you think of ways to improve the health of the wetland? Make a list and share it with a local conservation agent. Some of the items on your list might involve activities that you can do yourself. Would it help to pick up litter or clear away limbs and rocks that block water flow? If you do find a chemical source of contamination, report it to your local conservation office immediately.

Figure 10 Checklist for Water Quality

Check the descriptions that apply. Consider the following aspects when you evaluate the "health" of the water in your wetland area.

Name of Observer _____ Wetlands Location _____ Date _____

Water's Appearance
- ☐ clear
- ☐ muddy
- ☐ yellowish
- ☐ milky
- ☐ foamy
- ☐ oily
- ☐ scum
- ☐ other _____

Vegetative Cover
- ☐ 70–100%
- ☐ 30–70%
- ☐ 0–30%

Aquatic Life
- ☐ birds
- ☐ snakes
- ☐ fish
- ☐ insects
- ☐ worms
- ☐ crayfish
- ☐ others _____

Algae
- ☐ occur in spots
- ☐ everywhere
- ☐ none

Land Use Nearby
- ☐ homes
- ☐ woods
- ☐ factories
- ☐ fields
- ☐ stores
- ☐ parking lot
- ☐ farms
- ☐ other _____

Barriers/Structures
- ☐ dams
- ☐ waterfalls
- ☐ ditches
- ☐ channels
- ☐ docks
- ☐ beaver dams
- ☐ fallen trees

Litter
- ☐ paper
- ☐ cans
- ☐ bottles
- ☐ tires
- ☐ large items
- ☐ garbage
- ☐ total of items _____

Odor of Area
- ☐ none
- ☐ musky
- ☐ rotten egg
- ☐ chemical
- ☐ other _____

Overal Health
- ☐ excellent
- ☐ good
- ☐ poor
- ☐ extremely poor

CHAPTER 4

Mud, Muck, and Moisture

CERTAIN TYPES OF WETLANDS SUPPORT specific kinds of animals and plants. The types of life-forms that thrive in a particular region give that area its distinctive character. Can you think of other phenomena that determine a wetland's character? Think of what is below you and what is above you. The soil and the atmosphere help fashion a wetland environment.

Exploring the Soil

Many wetland treasures and wonders are right under your feet. To the untrained observer, the soil may seem to be lifeless and dull. Nothing could be further from the truth. The wetland is actually rich in life and ever dynamic in its processes. The soil provides many benefits and services to wetland wildlife. In many ways, it determines the kind of interactions that can occur in an area.

Like many other natural elements,

soil often varies from one region to another. All wetland soil is supersaturated with water for at least part of the year. Besides water, it contains minerals, gases, plant parts, microorganisms, and rock particles. The amount and composition of these elements determine the soil's physical characteristics.

What kind of surprises lie beneath your feet? See what you can uncover by digging deeper into the underground world.

Gritty, Sticky, or Slick: How to Determine Soil Texture

Is the soil in the wetland you've been studying spongy, slick, or firm? Knowing the soil types present in a wetland makes it easier to keep track of any new soil coming into the area.

In the past, wetlands were often filled in. Knowing what soil types existed prior to the dumping can help you determine how dumping has affected the region. If you want to protect your wetland, it helps to know it well. You can start by recognizing its soil types.

For your first soil investigation you will need a hand lens, a gardening spade, resealable plastic bags, a permanent marking pen, and your journal. Once you have collected the materials, select sites in the wetland to collect soil samples. Choose sites at various distances from the water that support different types of plant life. In your journal, make a map that shows the areas you are sampling.

Use the spade to remove about 20 centimeters (8 in.) of topsoil from each site. Place the soil sample in one of the plastic resealable bags and label it with the date and location.

Examine your soil samples one at a time. Note whether the first sample contains pebbles, small rocks, or organic matter such as bits of leaves or small twigs. Then, rub the sample between your fingers. Does the soil feel wet, gritty,

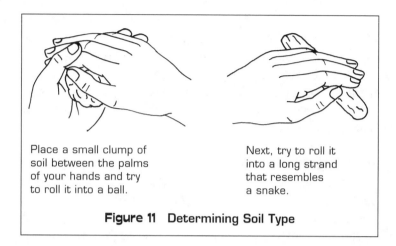

Place a small clump of soil between the palms of your hands and try to roll it into a ball.

Next, try to roll it into a long strand that resembles a snake.

Figure 11 **Determining Soil Type**

slick, dry, sticky? If it feels gritty, sand particles are present. If it feels like flour or talcum powder when dry, it is silty. Both silty and clay soils are slippery when wet. One example of a clay soil is kitty litter.

To differentiate between clay and silt, form a small ball about a centimeter in diameter. Roll the soil ball between your thumb and forefinger. If the soil holds together (forms a cast), try to roll it into a ribbon. See Figure 11. If you can easily roll it into a long, flexible ribbon, the soil probably consists mostly

Table 6 Sand, Silt, or Clay?

Soil Type	When Dry Soil Is Squeezed	When Wet Soil Is Squeezed
Sand	Falls apart when pressure is released	Forms as cast, but crumbles when touched
Silt	Forms a cast that can be handled freely without breaking	Forms a good cast, but cannot be rolled into a ribbon
Clay	Breaks into hard clods or lumps	Forms a thin ribbon

of clay. If it breaks easily, then the soil contains more silt than clay. Sandy soil and soil with large quantities of organic matter cannot be molded into a ribbon. See Table 6.

In your journal, note whether you think that clay, silt, gravel, sand, or organic materials are present at each site. Which is the dominant soil type in each sample? Do the samples vary from place to place?

✔ Doing More

For centuries, people have used clay to make decorative and useful items. Clay from wetlands can be used to make pottery and sculptures. Perhaps your art teacher can show you how to remove stones and other large particles from the clay.

Getting to the Core:
How to Make a Soil Profile

Top soil often looks very different from the soil farther down. Making a soil profile or cross section will let you see what the soil looks like at various levels below the surface.

A soil profile is a vertical cut into the soil that exposes the layerlike pattern of the soil. The layers shown in Figure 12 are called **horizons**. Each layer of soil has a characteristic color and texture. Just below the topsoil is an organic layer that consists of decomposing matter. The next layer, which has a high mineral content, is followed by a gray layer of loose sediment. Below this is a layer, called the gray mottled layer, with a high concentration of rootlets, and a rock layer known as the **parent rock**. In some areas, this layer is fairly close to the surface. The **water table** lies just below the parent rock. The layer beneath the water table is a solid rock layer called bedrock.

Begin by gathering a shovel, a ruler, and your journal and

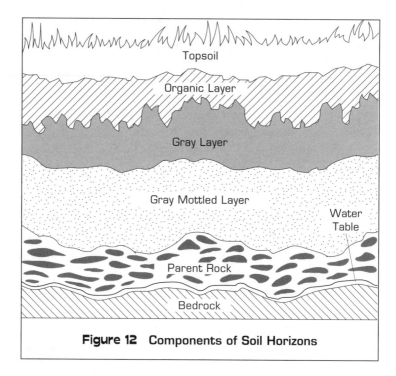

Figure 12 Components of Soil Horizons

heading out to a local wetland area. Select several spots for soil profiles. One could be a high spot; another could be a low area next to the water. Note the location of each site in your journal.

At the first site, carefully make a clean hole in the ground. It should be about 60 centimeters (24 in.) deep. In your journal, draw the layers or horizons that appear in your profile. Measure the height of each layer and note its color and texture. Look for any layers that contain organic material, rocks, or pebbles.

Your profile may include a layer of wet dark-brown or black soil called **hydric soil**. This layer will probably contain organic material and have a strong odor. It holds large quantities of organic matter because water-logged soil contains very little oxygen, and without oxygen, organic matter cannot decay.

If colors are present in wetland hydric soil, they are left

over from a time when the soil was dry and oxygen was able to combine with the metals in the soil. A reddish color indicates the presence of iron. Older wetland soil is usually gray.

If you do not see distinct soil layers, it is likely that soil from another site has been dumped in the wetland. Digging and transporting soil tends to cause mixing among the layers. Today, wetlands are protected from development by law. Most of them cannot be changed without going through several legal steps. In many cases, the wetlands must be left alone, undisturbed.

✔ Doing More

How acidic is the soil in your wetland area? You can find out by measuring the pH of each horizon. The soil in bogs tends to be very acidic.

Is there any correlation between soil's pH and its distance from the water? Compare a soil profile of the wetland with that of a well-drained location. Most fill material will come from a higher elevation so it will look very different from wetland soil.

Underground Creatures and Features: How to Identify Soil Components

By now you must have noticed differences in the texture, color, and appearance of the soil as you moved from one area of the wetland to another. Did you wonder what is responsible for these soil variations? Soil is a mixture of rocks, minerals, water, air, plants, and animals. The amounts of these components can vary. Some soil contains many types of insects, worms, and other organisms, while other soil is nearly lifeless. Scientists believe that there may be several million bacteria, fungi, and more than 100,000 protozoans in a single gram of some soils.

Table 7 Contents of Wetland Soil

Site	Depth	Texture	Soil Particles	Plants/Animals
1	Surface	Wet, sticky	Clay	Bits of stems and leaves
	10 cm (4 in.)			
	20 cm (8 in.)			
2	Surface			
	10 cm (4 in.)			
	20 cm (8 in.)			
3	Surface			
	10 cm (4 in.)			
	20 cm (8 in.)			

As you learned in Investigation 13, soil contains varying amounts of clay, silt, sand, and pebbles. In the following activity, you will be able to see and feel what makes up the soil in a local wetland area.

Before you begin, you will need a trowel or soil auger, a sorting screen, a teasing needle or toothpick, your journal, and a ruler. Instructions for building a soil auger and sorting screen are given in the Appendix.

Dig a hole about 10 centimeters (4 in.) deep. Spread the soil you removed in a thin layer on the sorting screen, and check its moisture by rubbing it between your fingers. In your journal, make a chart like the one shown in Table 7, and record how the soil feels—dry, wet, sticky, claylike, slippery. Also record information about the size and shape of the particles that make up the soil.

With a magnifying lens, check for living things such as worms, larvae, insects, and plant parts (stems, leaves and roots). Record these observations in the table.

Soak It Up:
How to Measure Soil Absorbancy

A wetland owes its existence in part to the soil that forms its base. The soil beneath any wetland receives all of its moisture from surrounding areas. The moisture is held in a wetland area because the soil at the bottom of the wetland is watertight or **impermeable**. Figure 13 will give you an idea of what permeable, semipermiable, and impermeable soils look like.

To find out just how permeable the soil is in a nearby wetland, you will need four sheets of clear acetate (like those used as overhead transparencies or term-paper covers), some rubber bands, a measuring cup, water, rulers, a stopwatch or a watch with a second hand, and your journal.

Begin by selecting four sites that may have different types of soil. Note the kinds of plants growing in each area. Describe the soil as well as you can in your field journal. Findings from Investigations 13–15 will come in handy.

Clear away the debris from a 5-centimeter (2-in.) square

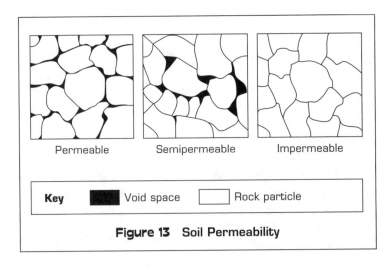

| Permeable | Semipermeable | Impermeable |

Key ■ Void space □ Rock particle

Figure 13   Soil Permeability

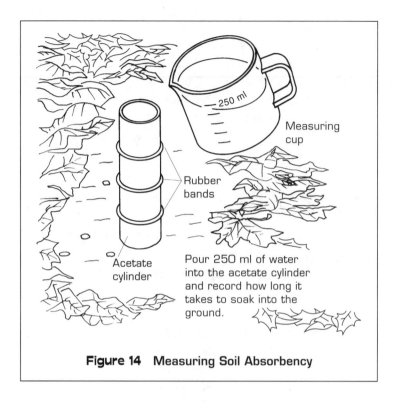

Figure 14 **Measuring Soil Absorbency**

area at each site. Roll up one sheet of acetate and place several sheets of rubber bands around the roll. (Measure and record the diameter of the roll and use the same size roll at each collection site.) Place the rolled acetate over the cleared soil, and push it gently into the ground, as shown in Figure 14.

The race is about to begin! Pour 250 milliliters (1 cup) of water into the acetate, and time its rate of absorption into the soil. If it takes a very long time for 250 milliliters to soak in, repeat the experiment using 125 milliliters ($\frac{1}{2}$ cup) of water at a site nearby.

Repeat the procedure at the other three sites using the same amount of water. Do the same experiment at a site near your home or school. Compare the various times it took for the water to be completely absorbed. The soil from well-drained areas absorbs water much faster than moist areas do.

✔ Doing More

Most parts of the United States and Canada have completed surveys on local soil. Soil and Water Conservation District officers have information on soil profiles for your area. It may be interesting to compare the data you obtained in your investigations with information on the official soil maps.

Things Just Pile Up:
How to Measure Sedimentation Rates

Sedimentation is a major cause of river and wetland destruction. In the Mississippi Delta, the land is constantly being extended into the Gulf of Mexico. However, the constant influx of sediment will eventually fill an enclosed area, such as a pond. If this happens, the silt overflow may end up in the wetland.

To find out how much silt is carried into your wetland area, you will need a tape measure and ruler, stakes (wooden or steel), a hammer, your journal, and nail polish (to mark the ground's level on the stakes). Begin by locating a wetland where water flow occurs. To determine the size of the delta (deposits of sediment) that has been formed by incoming sediment, you must make all your measurements from a constantly identifiable point such as a large rock or a tree. Use your measurements to create a scale drawing of the delta.

Mark each stake with a number or letter. Then, place the stakes into the soil at the edge of the delta and pound them firmly into the ground. See Figure 15. Using nail polish, mark the level of the silt on each stake. Measure the distance from the top of each stake to the top of the soil, and record your findings. Your work is now completed until a good rain occurs.

Return to the site after the next rainfall. Can you still see the marks you made with nail polish? Measure the distance

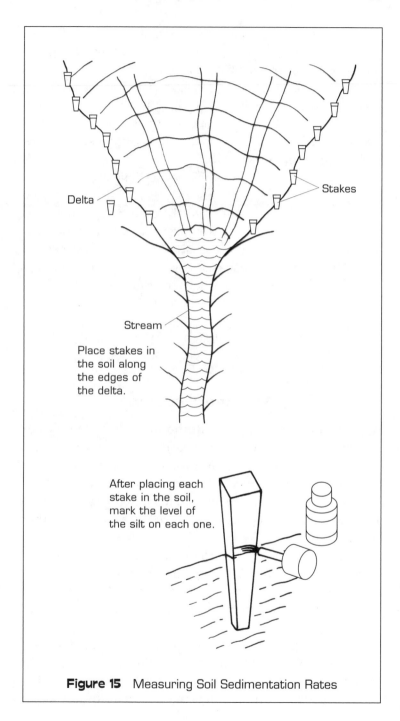

Figure 15 Measuring Soil Sedimentation Rates

from the top of the sediment to the top of each stake. Record your new findings in your journal. Compare these measurements with your original findings.

You may find that some of the stakes have been covered with additional sediment, while others are more exposed. Each rainstorm will produce different results. In some cases, additional sediment may be added. In other cases, old layers of sediment may be removed.

After each storm, mark the new sediment levels with a different color of nail polish. You may need to add new stakes as the delta gets larger—or smaller. Be sure to note any changes on your map. By watching the stakes through at least five or six rainstorms, you will be able to see the pattern in which sediment is deposited in your wetland. If you are in an area where it snows, how does the runoff after the spring snowmelt affect sedimentation deposits?

Wetland Weather

You could probably list all the ways that the weather influences many of your daily activities and affects your feelings. In the same way, but on a much larger scale, weather influences many components of a wetland environment. These aspects range from the types of life-forms that can thrive in a region to the types of soil that form there.

Weather is the condition of the atmosphere at a specified place and time. Major determinants of weather are the changes that occur in air pressure and temperature, wind direction and speed, and the amount of moisture in the air.

Do you want to be a wetland weather watcher? If so, then the activities that are presented in this section will help you acquire the necessary skills. Here's hoping that after these explorations you won't be "up in the air" about

meteorological conditions at the wetland site you chose to study!

INVESTIGATION **18**

Hot or Not? How to Assess Temperature Patterns

A wetland could not exist without the water that flows into it and remains there. In some cases, however, a wetland holds water for only a short time. Sometimes, the water disappears during the summer when the hot sun causes evaporation. While it is very difficult to determine the sun's precise effect on the wetlands, temperature variations are a good place to start.

For this exploration you will need your journal, five Celsius or Farenheit thermometers, five twist ties, and a long stick. (Before you begin, make sure that all the thermometers are displaying the same temperature.)

Place the thermometers in five diverse sites around the wetland. For instance, you may choose to place one in the cattails, another under a willow tree, and a third on an open mud flat. Find different types of sites for the other two thermometers too. Using twist ties, attach each thermometer to a stick, a plant, or a tree. Be sure that the thermometers are in roughly the same position—all hanging down, all in the shade, all at the same height. Give the thermometers a few minutes to stabilize, then record the temperature at each location. In your journal, make a table that includes the date and time, temperature, and weather conditions—amount of cloud cover, wind speed, and humidity. Use Table 8 as a guide.

Return to the wetland area once a week for the next several months to record temperatures and weather conditions. Does the sun and the resulting temperature affect the wetland you have chosen to investigate?

The greatest stress is placed on a wetland during July and August. If you do your investigation during these months,

Table 8   The Effect of Temperature on a Wetland

Site	Date	Time	Temperature	Weather	Type of water	Condition of plants
1	May 15	11:30 A.M.	37°C (80°F)	Partly sunny, breezy	Flowing stream	Green, healthy
2						
3						
4						
5						

the environmental factors that fatigue and affect the wetland will be at their harshest.

✔ Doing More

Compare water and soil temperatures recorded at several sites. Is there any correlation between these two sets of temperatures?

Water, Water Everywhere: How to Measure Soil's Water Content

Wetlands come in all sizes and shapes and they have all kinds of structures. Every one of those structures helps keep the water in the wetland. This exercise invites you to determine how much water a wetland's soil can hold. Try to collect samples from the wettest and driest parts of a wetland area. If the wetland contains peat or mossy areas, you could also select one of those areas for testing.

For this exploration, you will need a shovel, a cup, resealable plastic bags, a balance or scale, aluminum foil, and your journal. Choose several sites with different soils, and make a map of these locations in your journal.

Next, fill each cup with soil, pour it into a plastic resealable bag, and label each bag with the date and location. Fill the cup in the same way each time so that each sample will have the same volume.

When you get home, weigh each sample (including the plastic bag) on a balance. Note the mass of each sample in your journal.

Remove the soil and lay it on the plastic bag in direct sunlight. When it is completely dry, weigh each sample and note the dry mass in your journal. Subtract the dry mass from the wet mass to determine the water content of each sample.

If you want to be sure that you have removed absolutely all of the water, place the samples on labeled sheets of aluminum foil and dry them in the oven (at 200°F) for about 10 minutes. After the samples have cooled, pour the soil samples back onto the plastic bags and reweigh them. Look over your data to determine which of the soil samples has the greatest capacity to hold water.

✔ Doing More

Compare the wetland samples to samples collected from forests or dry land. Does soil with large quantities of organic mater or minerals hold more water or less water than other soil? What do your results tell you about one of the functions of wetlands?

CHAPTER 5

Mysteries of the Marsh: Use of Wetlands

THE BIOLOGICAL, GEOLOGICAL, AND physical aspects of a wetland play a role in determining its unique characteristics. Another factor that comes into play is how the wetland has been used by humans.

In this chapter, you will delve into some cultural, historical, and economic aspects of human use of wetlands. The following investigations will allow you to experience the special features, festivities, food, and financial characteristics of wetland areas!

Commercial fishing boats, such as the one shown here, collect huge quantities of fish and shellfish from wetlands each year.

How Green ($$) Is Your Wetland?
How to Assess the Value of a Wetland

To many people, "What's it worth?" means "How much money can I get?" Money is an important aspect of many plans and transactions, and financial concerns enter many land-use decisions. Only recently have humans begun to understand the economic value of wetlands. Wetlands provide flood protection, flood storage, nutrient storage and cycling, pollution filtering, wildlife habitats, storm-damage buffer zones, agricultural output, and a site for recreational activities.

Calculating the exact monetary value of each of these services can be challenging. Think of some of your own favorite things—they may be worth a lot to you, but other people may not consider them at all valuable. In nature, too, some values are impossible to assess.

Wetlands can contribute to culture by inspiring writers and artists. They may even be therapeutic, reducing the stress levels of people who visit them. Wetlands also provide ideal conditions for scientific research.

Could you assign a dollar-and-cent value to these uses? Because the importance of a wetland is often based on an individual's personal value system, it is difficult put a price on it. Despite this difficulty, some data do exist on wetland-related financial gains. For example, we know that commercial and recreational fishing in wetland areas is a multibillion-dollar industry because receipts and ledgers are available for fish and wildlife harvested from wetlands.

How much do you think the wetland you have been studying is worth? In general, a wetland area that can be used in a variety of different ways is more valuable than one that has fewer uses. The following activity will give you a rough idea of a local wetland's value. Even though this is just a crude way of thinking about the wetland's money-making potential, you can use it to show other people the value of a wetland.

Figure 16 Determining a Wetlnad's Value

Place a tally mark in all the columns that apply.

Name of Observer_____ Wetlands Location_____ Date_____

Use	Present	Past	Future	Comments
Aquaculture	☐	☐	☐	
Pollution	☐	☐	☐	
Scientific research	☐	☐	☐	
Hiking	☐	☐	☐	
Wildlife habitat	☐	☐	☐	
Plant harvesting	☐	☐	☐	
Hunting	☐	☐	☐	
Sport fishing	☐	☐	☐	
Commercial fishing	☐	☐	☐	
Migratory stopover	☐	☐	☐	
Mineral extraction	☐	☐	☐	
Flood control	☐	☐	☐	
Nutrient cycling	☐	☐	☐	
Sediment control	☐	☐	☐	
Water recharge	☐	☐	☐	

To conduct this study, you will need your journal, copies of Figure 16 and records of how the wetland has been used in the past. Start by contacting the owner of the wetland. You should also call a Soil and Water Conservation officer in your region. (The phone number will be in the Blue Pages.) Ask to interview a land specialist about the past uses of the wetland area you are studying. You could use the items in Table 9 as one way to begin the interview. Tally and record any comments under the past and present columns.

Also ask the land specialist or a local ecologist whether the land could potentially be used in other ways. If so, record these possible uses in the "Future" column. Compare the possible uses of this area with those of another wetland. Formulate your own position on the economic value of wetlands.

Point the Way: How to Use Plants as Indicators of Water Depth

How can you tell where something is located without actually seeing it? In wetlands, you can often identify areas that have water under the surface without digging down to see. Plants are excellent indicators of how much water is below the surface of the soil.

Certain plants, called **phreatophytes**, grow only in areas where their root systems can reach the **water table**. Thus, the presence of phreatophytes indicates that the water table is very close to the surface. Each region of the world has its own phreatophytes. Local well drillers, farm advisors, or agriculture extension agents can provide you with information about phreatophyte populations in your area.

When you go out to look for water-indicating plants, take identification books with you. Table 9 lists some of the plants you might find. As you locate each indicator plant, make a

Table 9   Distance to Water

Water Location	Plants
Just below the ground	Rushes, sedges, and cattails
Less than 3 meters (10 ft.) below ground	Reeds and cane, bamboo, willow, elderberry, birch, sycamore, alder bay, oak (Pickleweed and salt bush usually grow in arid or desert areas, but both can, and often do, grow in salty water.)
Less than 7 meters (23 ft.) below ground	Cottonwood, sycamore, arrow weed
More than 7 meters (23 ft.) below ground	Thick stands of rabbitbrush, black greasewood, mesquite

note of it in your journal. Also list the general characteristics of the surrounding land and plants. For instance, if you come across a grove of cottonwood trees, you can deduce that there is probably more water in this area than in another area where you find just one cottonwood tree.

Incredible Edibles: How to Prepare Foods from Wetlands

Sometimes the best food can appear in the least likely places! Wetlands provide an abundant source of nutrients for wildlife. They can also provide you with a variety of foods—fish, seafood, and a wide assortment of plants. The following projects present some easy recipes that feature wetland plants. Happy cooking and eating!

For each of the next three activities, you will need a large pot, knives, and scissors. You will also need some plastic bags for collecting plants from wetland areas. Your parents or friends can help cook and eat what your have collected.

Before eating plants that are submerged or in direct contact with water, find out about the quality of the water in which they are growing. Also, be sure that you are collecting plants that are safe to eat. Ask a local botanist to help you identify wetland plants.

PROJECT **8**

Vegetable du Jour: Cooked Cattails

Locate a spot where you can walk or wade into a colony of cattails (*Typha latifolia*). To collect a cattail, grasp the plant's stem firmly at a point close to the ground, and pull it up. The stem should break free from the roots fairly easily. Fifteen to twenty stems will provide a nice vegetable dish for your family and friends. Make sure that you do not remove all the cattails growing in one part of a wetland area.

When you get home, wash the cattails thoroughly, cut off the top 15 to 20 centimeters (6 to 8 in.) of stem, and discard the rest. Now peel away the outer leaf from the white central core of plant tissue. Sample the stems to check their tenderness. If the tissue is chewy, strip another layer of leaf from the round cylindrical stem.

Place the white cattail stems in a pot of water, add salt and butter, and bring the pot to a boil. Follow the directions in a cookbook for preparing asparagus. You can prepare a cheese sauce or cream sauce to pour over the cattails, or simply serve them with a little butter and enjoy the flavor. Cattail stems can also be eaten raw as a snack or in a salad. Do you think it would be a good idea to include cattail stems at the local salad bar?

Cattails are one of the most common types of emergent plants. They have distinct brown, flower spikes that contain thousands of tiny flowers.

Delicana Americana: Cattail Cobs

In early spring and summer, cattails develop green flower spikes. As they emerge, a papery sheath, like a corn husk, is visible. As the familiar cattail **catkin** grows and matures, the sheaf will be reduced and fall away. Collect the flower spikes when they are just a few days old—older spikes will be tough and chewy. This food was a favorite of early Americans; will it be one of yours?

Using a knife, cut the spikes and about 5 centimeters (2 in.) of stem. You can use the stem portion as a handle when you eat your tasty tidbit.

When you get home, wash the spikes thoroughly. Follow the instructions in a cookbook for preparing corn on the cob. Place them in boiling water and let them cook for about 8 minutes.

You can also place the spikes in a plastic bag and heat them in the microwave for a few minutes. *Be careful not to burn yourself. The spikes can get very hot.* Eat the spikes as you would eat corn on the cob—with lots of butter.

Nasturtium Melody:
Watercress Delights

Watercress (*Nasturtium officinale*), a water plant with many small leaves, is found in many gravel streams throughout the United States and Canada. Watercress usually develops roots on shore and grows out into the water, sometimes in large mats. This plant is a relative of mustard and nasturtium, which is grown in many home flower gardens. It was brought to the United States from Iran.

Crushed watercress has a very distinct scent and taste

Table 10 Recipes with Watercress

Use	Directions
Salad	Watercress can be used with a variety of greens. Add a small amount the first time to see if you like the taste with lettuce or spinach.
Stir-fry	Try watercress in a stir-fry meal. Chop it up and stir it into the rest of the vegetables. Adding ginger root can further enhance the flavor.
Omelette	Blending the watercress into your favorite omelette is easy. Chop the leaves and add the watercress, along with mushrooms or other tasty items, to beaten eggs and milk.

Watercress form large masses along the surface of streams. If you crush a leaf, you will be able to detect a pungent odor.

that adds a delicious flavor to a salad, soup, or stir-fry. Is your mouth watering yet? Then, it's time to collect some watercress.

When you get home, wash the plant thoroughly and place it in a cold, diluted solution of bleach for 30 minutes to remove any impurities. (A teaspoon of bleach in 2 liters [0.5 gal.] of water is adequate.) You may also wish to boil the water containing the watercress. Now you can use the watercress in any of the ways listed in Table 10.

CHAPTER 6

People, Problems, and Promises

More than 50 percent of the wetlands in the continental United States have been irreversibly altered or destroyed. You are fortunate to have been able to visit and explore wetland areas. This may not have been possible without the efforts of groups of environmentalists and concerned citizens. Many people have dedicated many hours to protecting and preserving wetlands.

Is there anything that you can do to make sure that future generations can explore wetlands just as you did? Yes. You can use the knowledge and experiences that you have gained to help protect and safeguard this important ecosystem. The activities presented in this chapter will help you work toward this goal. Remember, you can make a difference.

illegible handwritten scribble

Surveying the Situation:
How to Conduct a Survey

How often have you been asked, "What do you think?" Too often? Not often enough? Asking people about their attitudes and opinions can help you understand what they value and respect. If you understand what motivates people, you can usually understand their actions. If you are curious about what other people think about wetlands, then this is the activity for you.

Begin by reading the items on the survey shown in Figure 17. Do you think it is thorough? You may want to include additional questions. But, remember that if you make the survey too long, people will be less likely to fill it out.

Make at least twenty copies of your survey and decide how you would like to administer it—by phone, through the mail, or in person. Depending on the method you choose, you may want to use a tape recorder to keep track of comments from the people you interview.

When scientists conduct a survey, they try to choose subjects who represent all the different types of people in society. Political surveys try to include people from a variety of different ethnic backgrounds, different social classes, and different educational backgrounds. This diversity makes the survey more accurate. You should try to include as diverse a sampling of people as you can in your survey, too.

When you contact subjects, first identify yourself. Then state your interest in their views and ideas about wetland areas. Be courteous and appreciative with each individual.

If you administer the survey by phone, note each person's responses on a separate survey form. If you hand deliver the surveys, include an envelope for the completed survey and assure each person that all the information you collect will remain anonymous.

When all your survey forms have been completed, begin

Figure 17 Wetland Survey

Please answer each question as best as you can.

1. Age

☐ 6–12 ☐ 19–25
☐ 13–15 ☐ 26–40
☐ 16–18 ☐ 41–60
  ☐ 61+

2. I live in

☐ a city
☐ the suburbs
☐ a rural setting

3. I often participate in the following water-related activities. (Please ckeck all that apply.)

☐ fishing ☐ hiking
☐ boating ☐ birding
☐ swimming ☐ biking
☐ snorkeling ☐ other_____

4. I have visited the following areas. (Please check all that apply.)

☐ ocean ☐ bay
☐ lake ☐ bog
☐ pond ☐ river
☐ marsh ☐ swamp

5. Check the category that best describes your view.

Agree	*Disagree*	*Don't know*	
☐	☐	☐	Wetlands should be protected.
☐	☐	☐	Humans depend upon wetlands.
☐	☐	☐	Wetlands are worth much money.
☐	☐	☐	I know a lot about wetlands.
☐	☐	☐	The United States has plenty of wetland areas.

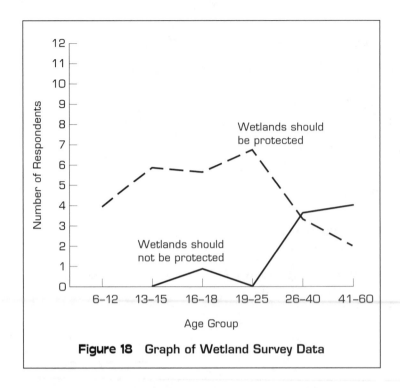

Figure 18   Graph of Wetland Survey Data

tallying the responses. Count up how many people gave a particular response to each question. For example, how many
people between the ages of 6 and 12 filled out the survey?
This may become a little more complicated for questions 3
and 4 because subjects may choose more than one answer.

Use a table to keep track of how people responded to the
questions on your survey. When you have counted all the responses, you can create graphs to show any patterns. Which
age group was the most likely to say that wetlands should be
protected? Which was the least likely? To answer this question, plot age on the x-axis and responses to question 5 on
the y-axis. See Figure 18. The answer will become obvious as
soon as you have plotted your data. You could also plot age
versus knowledge about wetlands, and where subjects live
versus how valuable they consider wetlands.

Wetland: Past and Future

You are a citizen not only of your country, but also of the planet. Responsible citizens make a point of being familiar with local issues, including those related to local ecosystems such as wetlands. If you contact the Planning and Zoning Departments in your town or city, you can learn what plans your local government has for the wetland areas in your community.

First, schedule a time to phone or visit your local Soil and Water Conservation official or a member of your community's zoning board. The phone numbers of these officials will be listed in the phone book under government offices. Ask the officials if there are—or ever were—plans for changing or developing local wetland areas.

If the answer is yes, ask some of the following questions:

- What was the nature of the proposed use? (housing, farming, etc.)
- How much land would be changed?
- What effect would the change have on animal and plant communities, sound levels, water quality, soil structure, and human population?
- What would be the short-term as well as long-term effects on the neighboring environment?
- Does the action meet the standards of your state's wetland regulations?

When you have the answers to these questions, identify the issues involved. For example, should the wetland be drained for purposes of highway construction? List all the short- and long-term benefits and risks involved with that action. If the proposed action conflicts with state wetland-protection laws, you need to decide what type of action you should take.

You could try to persuade the parties involved to ac-

knowledge your views and devise plans for resolving the differences. Political action could also be taken. You could write
to or contact local or federal government officials. Before you
begin any of these actions, make sure that all of the information you have is reliable so that you can defend your views.
Your actions can make a difference!

PROJECT **11**

Working for the Wetlands: How to Act for the Wetlands

Many people believe that each of us has a responsibility to
nurture and protect Earth. What can you do? You could take
the time to restore part of the wetland so that animals may
return to this environment in the future. You could also re-
plant an area to provide a new home for a water-loving
species. If you are willing to take on the task of helping your
wetland, the actions listed in Table 11 could be helpful in guid-
ing you.

Table 11   Ways to Help a Wetland

Action	Description
Write letters	Choose a group of people who needs to be in-formed about the problems or needs of the wetlands. You could write to the editor of the local newspaper, local or state government of-ficials, members of Congress, zoning board members, or local environmental clubs.
Develop a petition	Develop a petition and gather signatures of local citizens. Deliver the signed petition to the proper authority.

Table 11 (continued)

Action	Description
Take others to your site	Serve as a role model by involving other students or younger children in wetland protection. Adults will see your efforts to share the wetland with others as a positive action.
Write and publish a newsletter	One way to provide a large group of people with information is to write a newsletter. Using a word processor, write about your ideas and concerns. Make copies and hand them out to people who live in your area.
Plan and carry out a cleanup day	Ask your family and friends to help cleanup a local site. Ask a local grocery-store owner to provide garbage bags. Arrange for the city or a local agency to pick up the trash. Let the media know what you are doing.
Plan a project to improve the wetland	Conduct a survey to discover what can be done to improve the condition of a local site. Call local agencies to get help. University herbariums and agencies may provide plants that can be added to your wetland.
Plan for on-site improvements	You may want to add a nature trail, viewing sites, nesting platforms, or duck boxes; enlarge a pond; build erosion controls; or construct signs. You may be able to get the money you need for tools and materials from local businesses. When you come up with a plan, ask some friends or family members for help. After you have volunteers, begin to solicit local businesses for donations.
Attend meetings of organizations that affect wetlands	Becoming knowledgeable about the public's opinion on wetlands is critical. You must know how the community looks at your wetland before you undertake efforts to protect it. If the local zoning and planning committee is not aware of the value of wetlands, then you should educate them. Asking questions at a

Table 11 (continued)

Action	Description
	city council meeting or talking to your alderperson can place you in a position to improve a local wetland area. Invite these people out to the wetland so that they can see what you have done and what is needed.
Help control water-pollution in your wetland	Water entering your wetland may be carrying toxic materials, heavy sediment loads, or even raw sewage. On the other hand, your wetland waters may be very clean. You must know condition of the water in your wetland before you can begin any formal planning. If a stream flows through the wetland, follow its entire length and note any abnormal areas. Walk along each of the channels that enters the wetland and look for any strange deposits left by the water flow. Does the inflow come from a parking lot or business? Does it smell different? Make notes as you go and develop a plan for stopping the pollution from entering. Sometimes a good cleanup helps water quality. When you have data, find a group or a person to help you influence the people who control the wetland area.

Tools and Equipment

Exploring a wetland can be a real adventure. A few types of tools and equipment can make your explorations even more interesting and fun. This chapter describes equipment you can probably find around your home or at a local store. It also provides some directions for designing and constructing other types of equipment.

The following items are useful for collecting samples or for conducting investigations in a wetland area:

- collecting bottles (old peanut butter or jelly jars);
- thermometers;
- magnifying lenses;
- forceps;
- a dip net from an aquarium;
- a garden trowel;
- aquatic plant and animal identification books;
- other materials you can make using the directions in this chapter.

The following items can be made and used in a variety of wetland areas. Consider yourself a new architect of wetland collecting equipment!

Collecting/Sweep Net

You can create a sweep net to catch butterflies, dragonflies, and other terrestrial creatures. To change this

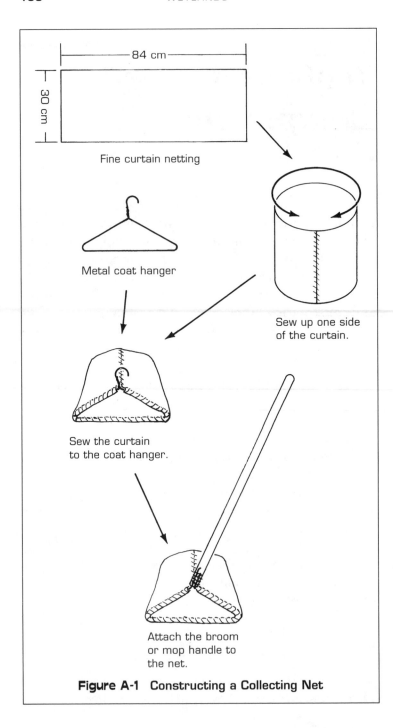

Fine curtain netting

Metal coat hanger

Sew up one side
of the curtain.

Sew the curtain
to the coat hanger.

Attach the broom
or mop handle to
the net.

Figure A-1 Constructing a Collecting Net

net's use, just bend it from a circle to a triangle. The triangular shape allows you to dip the net into a body of water along the bottom.

You will need a mop or broom handle, a heavy coat hanger or other wire (hardware or lumber stores have heavy gauge wire for this purpose), sheer curtains measuring 30 centimeters × 84 centimeters (12 in. × 33 in.), a heater-hose clamp from an auto-parts store, a sewing machine, scissors, and a screwdriver. Begin by cutting the coat hanger or wire; so that you have a piece with a round diameter. Also, cut off the hooked end of the coat hanger.

Then, sew the two sides of the curtain together, as shown in Figure A-1. Insert the coat hanger or heavy wire into the part of the curtain where the curtain rod is usually placed. Next, sew around the coat hanger so that it stays in place. Sew the other end of the curtain to complete the net. Now, attach the the mop or broom handle with the hose clamp and start swooping for insects! The net can also be used to collect underwater critters.

If you get the net wet, place it in a location where the water can evaporate from the netting. If you do not so this, mildew and mold will attack and destroy the netting material.

Bottom Viewer

Looking for critters under water can be difficult, but you can build a device that will make it easier to spot them. A bottom viewer can help you to gaze into the underwater world.

To build a bottom viewer, you will need a white bleach bottle or gallon-sized milk jug, heavy plastic wrap, a strong rubber band, a knife, and scissors.

Begin by cutting a hole about 2 centimeters (1 in.) from the edge of the container's bottom, as shown in Figure A-2. *Be careful not to cut yourself. Ask an adult to help if the container is too thick to cut easily.*

Cut a piece of plastic wrap 10 centimeters (4 in.)

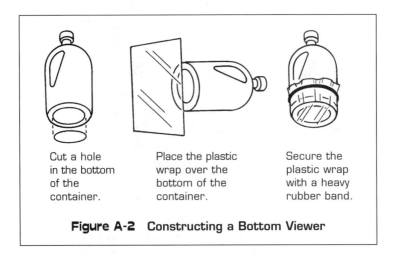

Cut a hole in the bottom of the container.

Place the plastic wrap over the bottom of the container.

Secure the plastic wrap with a heavy rubber band.

Figure A-2   Constructing a Bottom Viewer

longer and wider than the bottom of the container. Place the plastic wrap over the bottom of the container, and secure it with the rubber band. Remove the cap from the container. This opening becomes the eyepiece. Lower the other end into the water and see what swims by or scoots along the bottom!

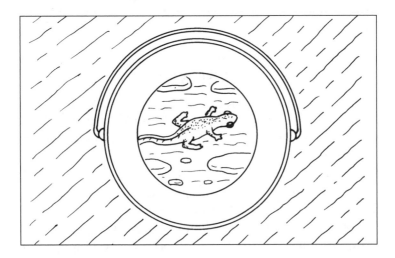

When you look a bottom viewer made from a bleach bottle, milk jug, or bucket, you should be able to see all sorts of plant and animal life.

A similar device can be made by removing the bottom from an old bucket. This viewer allows more people to see under the water.

Sampling Pan

S ampling pans can be used to hold the materials that you have gathered with your collecting net. To make sampling pans, collect several white bleach bottles, a permanent black marker, scissors, and a strong rubber band. Place the rubber band around the bleach jug (about 2 centimeters [1 in.] from the bottom). As shown in Figure A-3, draw a line just above the entire circumference of the rubber band.

Cut along the line on the container. *Be careful not to cut yourself. Ask an adult to help if the container is too thick to cut easily.* Next, number each pan on its side. As you collect a sample, write the number and your location on the pan. This will help you keep track of where each sample was collected. You can dump everything into this pan. The white bottom shows plainly the small organisms that live in wet areas.

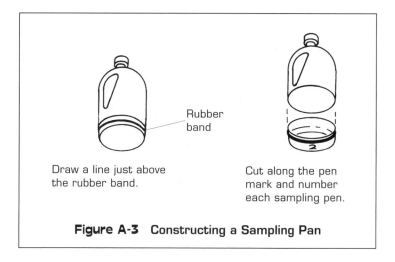

Draw a line just above the rubber band.

Rubber band

Cut along the pen mark and number each sampling pen.

Figure A-3 **Constructing a Sampling Pan**

Algae Sampler

Looking at algae under a microscope is interesting because there are so many different types. However, you must give the algae time to settle so that you can collect and observe them. The following device will allow you to collect samples.

To make your algae sampler, you will need a brick, a large plastic disk (such as the lid from a coffee can) three

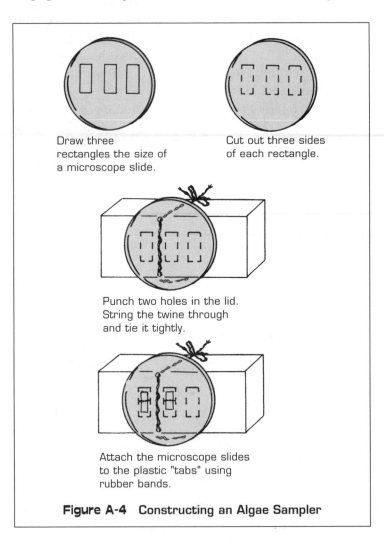

Draw three rectangles the size of a microscope slide.

Cut out three sides of each rectangle.

Punch two holes in the lid. String the twine through and tie it tightly.

Attach the microscope slides to the plastic "tabs" using rubber bands.

Figure A-4 Constructing an Algae Sampler

microscope slides, three rubber bands, and twine. On the plastic lid, draw three rectangles the same size as a microscope slide. As shown in Figure A-4, cut out *three sides* of each rectangle. The result will be three "tonguelike" tabs.

Next, punch two holes in the lid and string the twine through them. Wrap the twine around the bottom of the brick and tie it. The lid is now securely attached to the brick. Using a rubber band, attach a microscope slide to each plastic tab.

Now you are ready to place the algae sampler in the water. After a few days, remove the sampler. *Carefully* remove each rubber band by lifting it straight up and sliding it off. ***Do not scrape the rubber band across the surface of the slide.*** If you do, you will also scrape off the algae sample. View each slide under a microscope. (Ask a science teacher if you can use one of the school's microscopes.) In your journal, draw and describe what you found.

Sorting Screens

Sorting screens are useful for separating what you find in muck, gravel, or sand from the bottom of wetland areas. By running these samples through screens of different sizes, you can identify and group your discoveries more easily. Fossil collectors use such screens to remove big pieces of material and sort out their finds.

To construct the sorting screens, you will need strips of wood (four per screen) that are about 15 centimeters (6 in.) long, 15-centimeter × 15-centimeter (6-in. × 6-in.) squares of screening with different sizes of mesh or hardware cloth, a stapler, nails, and a hammer. (Workers at construction sites may give you the wood for the screens free. Just ask!)

Using the hammer and nails, join four wood strips together to form a square frame. ***Be careful not to hit your fingers with the hammer.*** Staple a piece of mesh over the

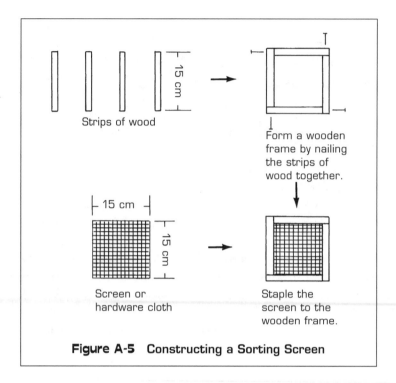

Figure A-5 Constructing a Sorting Screen

frame, as shown in Figure A-5. You can use these screens to sort both dry and wet materials.

Soil Auger

A soil auger can be used to gather soil samples without disturbing a large area of wetland. To collect a sample, clear away a small area, place the auger on the surface of the soil, and step on it so that the auger "cuts" into the soil. When you lift up the auger, you will also pull up a cross section of wetland soil.

To build a soil auger, you will need a tennis-ball can (a metal one works better), wire, an old tennis ball, scissors, a mop handle, masking tape, a hammer, and a nail. Begin by cutting out both ends out of the tennis-ball can. As shown in Figure A-6, poke two holes near the bottom of the can and string the wire through the holes to make a handle. Knot the ends of the wire that are inside the tube a few times to make them secure. Attach the wire to the sides of the can with masking tape.

Next, cut the tennis ball in half and nail it to the mop or broom handle. ***Be careful not to hit your fingers with the hammer.*** This device will act as a plunger. You can use it to remove a sample from the can so that you can examine it.

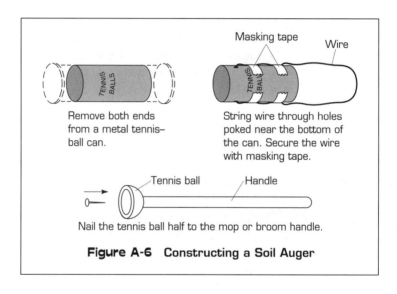

Remove both ends from a metal tennis-ball can.

String wire through holes poked near the bottom of the can. Secure the wire with masking tape.

Nail the tennis ball half to the mop or broom handle.

Figure A-6 **Constructing a Soil Auger**

Glossary

alluvial—an area where a fast-moving stream slows down. As a result, fine particles of sand or clay settle out of the water.

amphibians—a class of animals characterized by limbs without claws, slimy skin that lacks protective outgrowths, gills during some stage in the life cycle, numerous eggs usually laid in water, and a three-chambered heart.

anaerobic—living, active, or occurring in the absence of oxygen.

aquatic—growing or living in water.

asphyxiate—to suffocate, make unconscious, or kill an organism by blocking its oxygen supply.

biomass—living weight (mass) per unit area.

bog—a wetland formed when water backs up in a natural drainage area. Peat often builds up in bags.

budding—a form of asexual reproduction used by some simple organisms.

buoyancy—the tendency of a body to float or rise when submerged in a fluid.

calcareous fen—a type of wetland that is fed by alkaline water (high pH) from springs or seeps. All known fens in the United States are in glaciated areas. The plants that grow in calcerous fens are calcium lovers.

catkin—a tassel-like cluster of one-sexed flowers. Catkins occur on birches, cattails, and willows.

coniferous—plants that have sex organs in cones, have leaves in the form of needles, and are mostly evergreen. It is usually a tree or shrub.

detritis—small pieces of dead or decomposing plants and animals.

ecosystem—a community of organisms and their environment.

emergent plant—a plant with roots and part of its stem underwater. This type of plant can withstand flooding, but cannot live underwater for long periods of time.

estuarine wetland—wetland in which fresh water and salt water meet and mix. The water may be very shallow or very deep. Examples include salt marshes and mangrove swamps.

exotic plant—a plant species that is not native to the environment in which it is growing. One example is purple lustrife.

food chain—a sequence of organisms that transport energy derived from the sun. At the lowest level of any food chain is a plant, which converts the sun's energy into a form that is useful to animals. A herbivore is always at the second level of a food chain. Other animals in a food chain are carnivores.

food web—the complex network of feeding relationships in an environment.

free-floating plant—a plant that floats on the surface of the water. Its roots are not embedded in the soil below the water. Duckweed is one example of a free-floating plant.

gall—a growth on a plant that is caused by the irritation of another organism living within its tissue. Galls are caused by insects, fungi, and bacteria.

herbaceous—green and leaflike in appearance or texture, not woody.

herbarium—a collection of dried plants that have been identified and labeled; the room or building where a collection of plants is stored.

horizon—a layer of soil. Each horizon looks and feels different from the others. In most cases, it is possible to distinguish between two layers by looking at them.

hydric soil—soil characterized by, and showing the effects of, the presence of water.

hydrophytes—a plant that grows partially or completely submerged in water.

impermeable—does not allow water to move through.

indicator organism—an organism so strictly related to a particular environment condition that its presence is an indication that such a condition exists.

lacustrine wetland—a wetland associated with a lake, pond, or reservoir.

line transect—a sampling technique that inventories organisms along an arbitrary line.

mangrove swamp—a swamp characterized by tropical evergreen trees and shrubs that have stilt-like roots and stems. This type of wetland habitat often forms dense thickets along tidal shores.

marine wetland—a type of wetland found where the ocean meets the land. It is constantly exposed to salt water.

metamorphosis—the series of changes that some living things (such as insects) go through as they grow from egg to adult.

meteorological—having to do with the study of weather and climate.

migratory—the movement of animals from one area to another. The movement is often related to seasonal changes.

oxbow—a U-shaped bend in a river.

palustrine wetland—a wetland usually found in forested areas. Examples include bogs, marshes, swamps, or wet meadows.

parent rock—a soil horizon that contains rock.

peat—one of the simplest and most recently formed fossil fuels. It is soft, brown, partially decomposed plant-matter formed at the bottom of bog and marsh wetlands.

pH—a measure of the relative acidity of a substance. It is measured on a scale of 1–14, where pH 1 is the most acidic, pH 7 is neutral, and pH 14 the most basic.

phreatophyte—a deep-rooted plant that obtains water from the water table. These plants are often associated with dry areas and are used as indicators of water below the surface.

primary consumer—organisms that cannot make their own food and must get their energy by eating plants (producers). Cattle, sheep, and horses are examples of primary consumers.

producer—an organism, most likely a plant, that uses the energy of the sun to create its own food.

riverine wetland—a wetland found at the edge of a river or stream.

rooted floating plant—an aquatic plant with roots that extend into the soil beneath a body of water. The underwater portion of a plant provides support; draws minerals, oxygen, and water from the surrounding soil; and sometimes stores food.

salt marshes—a type of estuarine wetland that is dominated by grasses and grasslike plants. These marshes are common along the southeastern coast of the United States.

secondary consumers—organisms that cannot make their own food and must get their energy by eating primary consumers. Lions, dragonflies, and frogs are examples of secondary consumers.

sphagnum moss—pale or ashy mosses that decompose to form peat.

submerged plant—a plant that grows and reproduces entirely underwater.

succession/successional—the replacement of one community by another over time. The final stage of succession is a stable habitat known as a climax community.

symbiosis—a relationship between living organisms in which at least one benefits.

topographical map—a map that marks the variations in elevation across a landscape.

water table—the upper limit of the portion of the ground area that is completely saturated with water.

wetland—the area between dry land and deep water. It is characterized by the presence of water, saturated soils, and water-tolerant organisms.

wick—to carry away moisture.

wildlife inventory—an itemized list of organisms observed in a particular area.

For Further Information

Books

Hirschi, R. *Save Our Wetlands*. New York: Delacorte Press, 1994.

Lyon, J. G. *Practical Handbook for Wetland Identification and Delineation*. Boca Ratan: Lewis Publishers, 1993.

Lyons, J. and Jordan S. *Walking the Wetlands: a Hiker's Guide to Common Plants and Animals of Marshes, Bogs and Swamps*. New York: John Wiley and Sons, 1989.

McGavin, G. C. *Insects*. New York: Smithmark Publishers, 1992.

Niering, W. A. *National Audubon Society Nature Guides: Wetlands*. New York: Alfred Knopf, 1994.

Peterson, R. T. *Field Guide to the Birds*. 4th ed. Boston: Houghton Mifflin, 1980.

Williams, M. *Wetlands: A Threatened Landscape*. Oxford: Basil Blockwell Ltd, 1990.

Zim, H. *Insects*. New York: Golden Press, 1956.

Films and Videos

Fabulous Wetlands. Starring "Bill Nye, the Science Guy." Washington State Department of Ecology, Wetlands Section, Mail Stop PV-11, Olympia, WA 98504.

The Marsh Community. Encyclopedia Britannica Educational Corporation, 425 North Michigan Avenue, Chicago, IL 60611.

Conserving America: Wetlands. National Wildlife Federation, 1400 Sixteenth Street NW, Washington, D.C. 20036-2266.

Wetlands. Cooperative Extension Forestry and Wildlife Office, 103 Nutting Hall, University of Maine, Orono, ME 04469.

Why Wetlands? Federation of Ontario Naturalists, 355 Lesmill Road, Don Mills, Ontario M3B 2W8, Canada.

Internet Resources

Due to the changeable nature of the Internet, sites appear and disappear very quickly. These addresses offered useful information on wetlands at the time of publication.

About Wetlands
http://dino.ils.nwau.edu/wetlands/pages/about-wetlds.html

Interested in Wetlands
http://www.epa.gov/docs/Region4Wet/other.html

National Wetlands Inventory
http://www.nwi.fws.gov/ecology.html

U.S. Army Corp of Engineers Homepage
http://www.usace.army.mil/ j

Wetlands Activities
http://www.usgs.gov/fact-sheets/wetlands-activities/wetlands-activities. html

Wetlands and Endangered Species Regulation Center
http://www.wetlands.com/

Index

About the Authors

Marylin Lisowski is a professor of science and environmental education at Eastern Illinois University in Charleston, Illinois. She has taught at the elementary, middle-school, and high-school levels and was the director of a research station in the Bahamas. She was selected as Ohio's Outstanding Science Teacher of the Year, Florida's Honor Biology Teacher, and Illinois's Environmental Educator of the Year.

Robert A. Williams is a professor of science and environmental education at Southern Illinois University in Edwardsville, Illinois. A water, river, and wetlands activist, he directs the Rivers Project, a nationally recognized, interdisciplinary project for high-school students, and the Illinois Middle School Groundwater Project, which helps students study and protect well water and drinking water. Dr. Williams has co-authored a number of science books for early childhood educators and has been the recipient of numerous national awards.